Faithful&True

Faithful
&True

A Study Guide
to the Book of
Revelation

Greg Carey

the pilgrim press

The Pilgrim Press
700 Prospect Avenue East
Cleveland, Ohio 44115-1100
thepilgrimpress.com

Published 2022.

Unless otherwise noted, biblical quotations are taken from the New Revised Standard Version of the Bible, © 1989 by the Division of Christian Education of the National Council of Churches of Christ in the U.S.A., and are used by permission. Adaptations may be made for inclusivity.

Printed on acid-free paper.

26   25   24   23   22   1   2   3   4   5

Library of Congress Cataloging-in-Publication Data on file.
LCCN: 2021949944

ISBN 978-0-8298-2173-4 (paper)
ISBN 978-0-8298-2185-7 (ebook)

Printed in The United States of America.

I dedicate this study

to the memory of the

REV. RAYMOND F. LUBER, JR.,

and in honor of

SUZANNE J. LUBER.

I thank God for their support, their

encouragement, and their wisdom—

and most of all,

for their love.

CONTENTS

I | MAKING SENSE OF REVELATION

SUMMARY

Revelation intimidates many readers because of its striking symbols and depictions of gruesome judgment. Like other biblical books, Revelation was written for a group of real people in their struggle to lead faithful lives under challenging circumstances. And like other biblical books, Revelation speaks to us first by speaking to its own time and place. Understanding that Revelation belongs to a group of ancient Jewish and Christian "apocalypses" opens the path to our understanding.

BASIC BIBLE REFERENCES

Revelation 1

WORD LIST

Apocalypse
Dead Sea Scrolls
Eschatology
Asia (Roman province)
Witness/Testimony
Martyr
Patmos

MAKING SENSE OF REVELATION

I

Wild Enough

A dragon and two beasts. Creatures that resemble lions, oxen, eagles, and humans—and they speak! Hail and fire, mixed with blood; stars falling from the sky. Combat between the armies of heaven and their enemies.

If we were reading science fiction or a comic book, we might declare these images too confusing and give up on understanding the story. We might dismiss these fearsome beasts and cosmic portents as being in bad taste and ignore them. But because these dramatic images occur in the very last book of the Bible, and because they have exerted so much influence on our art and our culture, we give Revelation a chance. At least, that's what you're doing as you read this study guide.

Revelation's opening passages provide a great deal of information that should help us understand the book. They introduce the book as an "apocalypse," a form of literature that emerged two or three centuries before Jesus's birth. Because we have access to several great Jewish and Christian apocalypses, we know a good deal about how to understand Revelation. The first few verses introduce John, the author, and the seven churches to whom he is writing. We assume John wanted those ordinary believers, our ancestors in the faith, to understand his message—that gives us a chance, too! In this first chapter, John tells us a bit about his vision of the risen Jesus. His description of that encounter indicates the book's primary concern: What does the risen Jesus have to say to those seven churches?

No one is promising to decode every symbol, every number, or every strange happening in Revelation. Commentators try, but certainty is too much to ask. However, we have a strong chance to understand Revelation well enough that we may overhear God's word to us through this fascinating book.

Why Read Revelation at All? Common Objections

Before we begin to read Revelation directly, we should acknowledge that many people do not like the book. Objections to Revelation go back centuries, way back to the earliest days of "the Bible." Our New Testament began when early Christians made copies of their most treasured literature to share with one another. A church in one city might have had one Gospel and a few of Paul's letters, while another church might have had a copy of another Gospel and other letters. Naturally, these believers wanted to share these treasures with one another—enough to undertake the laborious and expensive process of making word-for-word copies and distributing them to one another. When churches began discussing which "books" were appropriate for public reading in worship, Revelation found itself sometimes included and sometimes excluded.

> The great psychologist C. J. Jung attributed Revelation's depictions of violence to "the outburst of long pent-up feelings such as can frequently be observed in people who strive for perfection" (1954, 125).
>
> The English literary genius D. H. Lawrence described Revelation as "the work of a second-rate mind" that "appeals to second-rate minds in every country and every century" (1995, 66).

In the modern age, concerns about Revelation have multiplied. Many readers object that Revelation voices a "pie in the sky" outlook. Offering hope for divine intervention in the future and a life in the New Jerusalem, some say Revelation provides little guidance or inspiration for living in the here and now. On the contrary, we shall see that Revelation was very much engaged with the present-day concerns of its ancient audience. It did not separate their spiritual lives from their social and political experiences. Revelation called those first-century Christians to "faithful witness" after the model of Jesus, even at the risk of their lives, and it critiqued cultural practices that were violent and exploitative. Indeed, today many readers around the world turn to Revelation as a resource for resisting injustice and idolatry.

Other readers object that Revelation promotes a violent imagination. We should not discount this criticism. Revelation features many scenes of gruesome judgment. It seems to divide the "saints" from what it calls "the inhabitants of the earth." One wonders whether Revelation envisions any hope that ordinary people might repent in the face of judgment (see 9:20–21; 16:9–11). Those who defend Revelation point out that the book calls its audience to faithful witness and endurance, not to violence. Moreover, the Lamb—Revelation's primary symbol for Jesus Christ—endures slaughter and "makes war" with the sword of his mouth. Nevertheless, we find no easy way to separate violent judgment from Revelation's message.

Some readers, too, point to how Revelation defines its female symbols in terms of their sexual status. Revelation presents "good" symbols like the woman clothed with the sun (chapter 12) and the New Jerusalem (chapters 21–22) as a mother and a bride, respectively, but "bad" symbols such as Jezebel (2:20–24) and Babylon (especially chapters 17–18) in terms of sexual promiscuity. One confusing passage refers to the Lamb's 144,000 followers as those "who have not defiled themselves with women" (14:1–5), language that raises all sorts of questions about gender and sexuality. Observing that biblical authors like Hosea and Ezekiel used sexual imagery to describe Israel's "involvement" with idolatry, Revelation's advocates maintain that its gendered language simply reflects standard metaphors and does not imply a negative view of women. Nevertheless, these images remain troubling, especially in view of the images of sexual violence that attend Jezebel and Babylon.

So, Revelation faces strenuous objections. Why should contemporary readers turn to it? For one thing, Revelation reveals the struggles one set of Christian communities—our spiritual ancestors—faced in their own time and place. In that respect, Revelation functions like Paul's epistles: we overhear this holy conversation in order to explore how Revelation might speak to our own questions and challenges. Also, Revelation plays a unique role in the New Testament canon. More than any other document, Revelation testifies that the risen Christ reigns over every system of authority and power. No simple political statement, Revelation's sharp critique of Roman domination challenges contemporary readers to discern how the church should relate to issues such as power, empire, and loyalty. Read with care, Revelation opens pressing conversations that remain relevant for believers throughout the world.

An Apocalypse

Revelation gets its name from its very first word: *apokalypsis*, the Greek word we translate as "revelation." As a result, many traditions refer to Revelation as "the Apocalypse." In ancient literature, an "apocalypse" referred to a revelation or an unveiling, an instance in which things that have been hidden come into plain view. In the biblical traditions, an apocalypse could refer to either an individual's mystical vision (as in Galatians 1:12 or 2 Corinthians 12:1–10) or to a specific literary form.

Jewish apocalypses seem to have emerged in the second or third century BCE. The book of Daniel represents the first apocalypse to find its way into our Bible, though parts of another Jewish apocalypse, *1 Enoch*, may be even older. The apocalypses include great Jewish works like *2* and *3 Baruch*, *4 Ezra*, and the *Apocalypse of Abraham*, along with Christian apocalypses such as the *Shepherd of Hermas*, the *Apocalypse of*

Peter, and the *Ascension of Isaiah*. Some of these books were quite popular. Among the Dead Sea Scrolls, an important collection of Jewish documents discovered in 1946, at least eleven copies of *1 Enoch* have been identified. The New Testament epistle of Jude actually cites Enoch as Scripture (Jude 14–15), and to this day the Ethiopian Orthodox Church includes *1 Enoch* in its canon. Meanwhile, for centuries *Hermas* rivaled Revelation in popularity in some Christian circles.

> Revelation is the New Testament's only true apocalypse, leading many readers to assume that it is unlike any other ancient literature. However, a few quotations from other ancient apocalypses may help us see Revelation as part of a much broader literary movement.
>
> *I, Daniel, saw in my vision by night the four winds of heaven stirring up the great sea, and four great beasts came up out of the sea, different from one another. (Daniel 7:2–3)*
>
> *On the second night I had a dream: I saw rising from the sea an eagle that had twelve feathered wings and three heads. (2 Esdras 11:1)*
>
> *. . . suddenly I saw an enormous wild beast, something like a sea monster, with fiery locusts spewing from its mouth. (Shepherd of Hermas, 22.6, in Ehrman 2003, 229)*

Though diverse, the literary apocalypses share many things in common—and Revelation is no exception. Apocalypses all tell stories: they narrate the visionary experience in which a seer explores eschatological mysteries. "Eschatology" involves "ultimate things"—secrets about the heavenly (and hellish) realms or the ultimate course of history. Apocalypses typically cloak their revelations in striking and mysterious images, numbers, and other symbols. Remarkably, all the apocalypses include an angelic mediator who guides the seer through the experience. Revelation begins by mentioning the angel who accompanies John (1:1).

The apocalypses also contributed some ideas that proved critical for the development of Judaism and the emergence of Christianity. Among those ideas are the hope for resurrection, the expectation of a final judgment, interest in evil spiritual forces such as Satan and demons, and speculation concerning a messiah. We might encounter hints of these ideas in the Jewish Scriptures, but they all developed markedly in the apocalypses.

Prior to Daniel, the Jewish Scriptures never mention a final judgment, nor do they clearly express an expectation for the resurrection of the righteous. Many apocalypses describe the present age as a time of mounting chaos, building toward God's decisive intervention to deliver the righteous and inaugurate an age of justice, peace, and prosperity. When Jesus delivers his "little apocalypse" (Mark 13; Matthew 25; Luke 21), he's drawing precisely upon the kinds of ideas that represent "apocalyptic eschatology," which concern the climax of history and a final judgment.

Interpreters have employed several images to help modern readers appreciate the apocalypses. Some compare the apocalypses to political cartoons. When modern Americans see an elephant squaring off against a donkey, they immediately discern that we're really talking about Republicans and Democrats. Likewise, the apocalypses employ grotesque beasts to portray Israel's imperialistic enemies (see Daniel 7 and Revelation 13). Sheep and lambs, good; dragons, bad.

It also helps some readers to imagine the apocalypses as a kind of poetry. Revelation, like several other apocalypses, demonstrates significant literary artistry. Its symbols weave back and forth, interacting with one another in significant ways. Revelation rarely quotes scripture verses, but it frequently draws upon words and images taken directly from Israel's prophetic literature. Just as poems create meaning through concentrated language and powerful imagery, so do the apocalypses.

A Letter

Revelation clearly indicates that it was addressed to real people who lived in a particular place and time. After introducing itself as an apocalypse and a prophecy (1:1–3), Revelation then slides into the form of a letter. The book addresses "seven churches" (1:4) in the Roman province of Asia—in current-day western Turkey—and very soon the risen Jesus addresses individual messages to these seven churches.

Revelation's identity as a letter indicates that the book spoke to the real-life concerns of first-century disciples. Christians who twist Revelation into a bizarre prediction of current events, "straight from today's headlines!", overlook the book's insistence that it was speaking to real people who would understand its message in their own time and place. Revelation insists that "the time is near" and that it describes things that must happen "soon" (1:3, 19; 22:6). In this respect, Revelation very much resembles other apocalypses of the day. It solves nothing to "spiritualize" this language in an attempt to turn Revelation into something it's not.

We'll learn more about those seven churches in our second session, but for now it's enough to know that as a letter Revelation offers guidance to early Christians who face significant challenges. John describes them as a priestly kingdom (1:6, 9), but they also fear persecution (1:9). They live in a context that makes faithful testimony to Jesus not only difficult but dangerous.

A Vision of the Risen Jesus

Revelation's first chapter concludes with a vision of the risen Jesus. John describes himself as being on the island of Patmos, about ninety miles from the mainland, "on account of the word of God and the testimony of Jesus" (1:9). Most interpreters think John has been exiled to Patmos, whether by local authorities or as an escape from danger, though we cannot be certain about this.

John's language, "the testimony of Jesus," suggests persecution. The Greek word *martyria*, translated as "testimony" here, generally refers to the kind of activity witnesses provide in a courtroom or civil hearing. But in Revelation *martyria* and related terms mean public testimony to Jesus—an activity that can lead to suffering and death. Revelation is the first work of Greek literature that uses *martyria* in this way: here a *martys* is a martyr (17:6). Revelation calls Jesus the "faithful witness" (1:5; 3:14); it also includes several references to believers who have given their lives in testimony to Jesus (2:13; 6:9; 11:7; 20:4). Revelation calls its audience to testify faithfully even in the face of death (12:11). We'll consider this feature of Revelation again in session two.

John describes a visionary experience: on the Lord's Day, John was "in the Spirit" when he heard a loud voice behind him commanding him to write (1:10–11). Experts debate whether Revelation represents an authentic visionary experience or a polished literary product that draws upon the standard elements of apocalyptic literature. It certainly shows literary artistry and design, though we cannot rule out the mystical possibility. Jews and Christians did prepare themselves for mystical encounters. In any event, the question of an authentic visionary encounter makes little difference for practical interpretation of Revelation.

The Jesus John encounters makes for a fearsome spectacle. The images in this scene largely derive from Daniel 7:9–18. Dazzlingly bright, with bizarre characteristics such as a sword protruding from his mouth, this portrait has defied those artists who have attempted straightforward representation.

The main points lie beyond our attempts to imagine what Jesus may have looked like in John's vision. First, this is no warm, domesticated Jesus who holds a lamb in one hand while patting children on the head with the other. No, his primary characteristic is intensity. Confronted by this overwhelming presence, John falls at Jesus's feet as if John were dead (1:17). This, too, is a standard motif in the apocalypses, as in Daniel 8:17.

Modern readers may recoil from the fearsome Jesus described here; however, if we remember Revelation's audience—small, vulnerable circles of disciples who face some sort of opposition—they need a fierce Jesus who can protect them. This leads us to a second point: the risen Jesus stands among seven lampstands while holding seven stars in his right hand. Jesus himself interprets these details: the seven lampstands represent the seven churches, the seven stars the "messengers" or "angels" of those seven churches (1:20). Commentators debate whether those seven messengers represent Christian leaders—perhaps the ones who would deliver John's message to the churches, or the actual heavenly representatives of those churches. In any case, we need no such precision to grasp the point. No matter how daunting the churches' circumstances, the glorious risen Jesus, so fierce in his intensity, dwells among them and holds their concerns in his powerful hand.

FOR FURTHER STUDY AND REFLECTION

Meditate

1. Revelation 1:9 tells us something about John's circumstances. After praying for the Holy Spirit's guidance, mindfully read this verse three times (aloud if you're able).

Research

1. Read Daniel 7 and Revelation 13. Notice where Daniel and Revelation use common language or images. Consider how Daniel and Revelation might reflect common outlooks on the world.

2. Online or in a good Bible dictionary like the *Eerdmans Dictionary of the Bible*, the *HarperCollins Bible Dictionary*, the *Anchor Bible Dictionary*, or the *New Interpreter's Dictionary of the Bible*, read an entry on "apocalypse" or "apocalypticism." How does familiarity with ancient apocalyptic literature help us understand Revelation?

Reflection

1. Revelation 1:5 refers to Jesus as "the faithful witness," and John claims he is on the island of Patmos on account of the "testimony of Jesus" (1:9). In what ways was Jesus a "faithful witness," and what might faithful witness mean today?

2. Revelation 1:9 mentions persecution. But the risen Jesus stands among the seven churches (1:20). Have you experienced Christ's presence among communities of believers who are under distress?

3. Can you recall an instance in which a work of art—poetry, fiction, music, or film—profoundly affected how you view the world?

2 | "TO THE ONE WHO CONQUERS"

Revelation and the Churches

SUMMARY

Before it presents its dramatic symbols and unsettling portents, Revelation speaks directly to the seven churches that comprise its audience. Though the book itself functions as a letter (Revelation 1:4), these seven letters speak directly to the individual churches, offering words of comfort, admonition, and encouragement. The letters vary only slightly from a common template, but they direct very specific messages to each one of the seven churches. These letters claim the highest level of authority, as they speak the words of the risen Jesus. Modern readers, far removed from the circumstances in which these letters were written, perceive that the letters speak to sharp divisions experienced among those churches.

BASIC BIBLE REFERENCES

Revelation 2–3

WORD LIST

Imperial cult
Admonition
Exhortation
Balaam
Jezebel
Nicolaitans

2 | "TO THE ONE WHO CONQUERS"
Revelation and the Churches

Having revealed the risen Jesus to its audience, Revelation does not plunge directly into beasts, trumpets, and other bizarre symbols. Instead, the risen Jesus dictates a series of seven letters, each one addressed specifically to one of the seven churches in Asia. The letters work from a common format, but each letter voices a specific message to a single church.

Many readers, especially historians, find in these letters our most helpful clues for understanding why John composed Revelation and what concerns this apocalypse was designed to address. The letters reveal some of the circumstances and tensions that faced early Christians in Asia, including debates about how best to follow Jesus faithfully under difficult circumstances. A solid grasp of the concerns reflected in these letters provides a key for understanding the rest of the book.

Seven Cities

Like most international movements, early Christianity grew as an urban phenomenon. Although Jesus and his disciples largely circulated in the villages and byways of rural Galilee, the international Jesus movement found it convenient to work through networks of cities. This holds for the seven churches of Asia.

And what cities! Tourists still flock to Ephesus for some of the most dramatic ruins left over from the Roman period. One of the top five Roman cities with a population of perhaps half a million inhabitants,

Ephesus possessed a famous temple to Artemis ("Great is Artemis of the Ephesians!"; Acts 19:28, 34)—one of the Seven Wonders of the Ancient World—a monumental library, and a theatre that seated 25,000 people. Pergamum was noted for its great altar, now on display in Berlin, and for its own fabulous library and 10,000-seat theatre. Below Pergamum was the Asclepion, a sort of hospital/spa dedicated to the god of healing. Smyrna, a port city like Ephesus, often competed with Ephesus and Pergamum for recognition from Rome. The other cities could not quite compete with Ephesus, Pergamum, and Smyrna, but Laodicea gained a reputation for banking, commerce, and administration. These Christians lived in some of the ancient world's most prominent cities.

Ancient cities competed for status within the Roman Empire. One of the most common vehicles for earning favor involved building shrines or hosting festivals in honor of the emperor or the imperial gods. We know the various temples and festivals devoted to the worship of Rome as the imperial cult. A city could not develop such an undertaking on its own any more than Atlanta or Shanghai may simply announce that it is hosting the Olympics. This process involved petitioning the Roman Senate for approval. We should not think that Rome imposed the imperial cult upon its citizens. Instead, the process involved at least two dimensions. (1) Local elites desired to demonstrate their gratitude to Rome and to enhance their public status, so they submitted bids for shrines and festivals, and (2) Rome reciprocated the cities' initiative by rewarding their requests—though such approval was not automatic.

The cities of Asia were especially well known for their devotion to the imperial cult. In 9 BCE, the provincial council of Asia announced a competition: the city that presented the emperor Augustus with the greatest honors would win a crown. Proclaiming Augustus as "Savior" for putting an end to war and announcing his birth as "the beginning of the gospel," the Asian council appointed Augustus's birthday as the perpetual New Year's Day. By the end of the first century CE, all seven cities hosted an imperial temple or imperial priests, with Ephesus and Sardis each hosting *two* sites of imperial worship in addition to temples devoted to individual emperors and the like.

We should imagine the Asian churches as small clusters of Jesus believers who made their way in these dynamic, multicultural, and religiously observant cities. Imagine dozens or a few hundred Christians in cities with tens of thousands, even hundreds of thousands, of inhabitants. It's that situation—small minority communities inhabiting major cities and surrounded by sites of worship dedicated to all the deities of the Roman world—that shapes the letters to the churches.

Common Format, Distinct Messages

"To the angel of the church in _____ write...." So begins each of the seven letters. The risen Jesus identifies himself to the church, speaks directly to that community and its circumstances, and offers a word of blessing or warning.

The seven letters all include a common set of elements. (1) They begin with an address: "To the angel of the church in _____ write," followed by a symbolic reference to Jesus. Most of these references point back to words from Revelation 1: the seven stars and lampstands, Jesus as first and last, the two-edged sword, the burning eyes and burnished feet, seven spirits and seven stars, the key, the faithful witness. All these symbols hold their own meaning, but they also demonstrate the larger unity of John's vision. (2) The letters address the circumstances of each individual church. Some churches are struggling while others seem to prosper; some churches are faithful while others waver. (3) The letters pronounce a word of comfort, admonition, or exhortation. Some churches are doing the best they can, especially those in difficult circumstances, and they receive comfort from the risen Jesus. But other churches require admonition, a word that combines warning with instruction regarding the correct path. Still other churches receive exhortation, the sort of encouragement one associates with a pep talk.

Each letter includes both (4) "Let anyone who has an ear listen to what the Spirit is saying to the churches" and (5) a promise for "the one who conquers," though the order varies.

CHURCH	ASSESSMENT	MODE OF ADDRESS	PROMISE
Ephesus (2:1–7)	enduring patiently "but I have this against you"	**Admonition:** remember, repent, do *if not . . .*	eat of the tree of life (2:7)
Smyrna (2:8–11)	persecution and poverty	**Exhortation:** do not fear	not be hurt by the second death (20:6)
Pergamum (2:12–17)	holding fast and not denying "but I have a few things against you"	**Admonition:** repent	hidden manna white stone new name (19:12)
Thyatira (2:18–29)	works greater than at the beginning "but I have this against you"	**Admonition/ Exhortation:** you'll get what you deserve hold on to what you have	power over the nations (19:15) morning star (22:16)
Sardis (3:1–6)	dead, though with a reputation for being alive some have not soiled their garments	**Admonition/ Exhortation:** awake, strengthen, remember, keep	clad in white (4:4; 6:11; 7:9, 13) book of life (20:12)
Philadelphia (3:7–13)	good works, kept my word little power	**Comfort:** an open door kept from the time of trial	written a new name (22:4) and of the New Jerusalem (21:2)
Laodicea (3:14–22)	lukewarm supposedly rich	**Admonition:** buy the true gold	sit with Christ on the throne (7:17)

As we see from this chart, the risen Jesus offers a different word for each of the churches, depending on their circumstances and their level of faithfulness. Comfort to Philadelphia, exhortation to Smyrna, admonition to Ephesus, Pergamum, and Laodicea, and a mixture of exhortation and admonition to Thyatira and Sardis.

Contemporary Christians might well reflect on this reality. Our cultural environment tends to reduce God to a Divine Butler, whose primary job description involves blessing people and keeping them happy. These letters paint a different picture. The risen Jesus has a distinctive word for each circumstance. Where the church is faithful, there's encouragement. Where the church suffers, there's comfort. And where the church is out of line, well, watch out!

Trouble in Asia

The letters to the churches reveal Christian communities that experienced pressure from within and from without. Most interpreters basically agree on the most essential problems the churches were facing.

First, pressure from without. As we have seen, Revelation is the first work of Greek literature to use the term *martys*—which usually denotes a witness in a legal setting—to mean "martyr." When Revelation identifies Jesus as the "faithful witness" (1:5), that is what it has in view: Jesus's faithful witness led to the cross. But in the letter to Pergamum, we encounter another "faithful witness," a man named Antipas "who was killed among you" (2:13). The letters also refer to persecution (2:9), to prison (2:10), and to endurance (or resistance—*hypomonē:* 2:2–3; 2:19). Later, Revelation will refer to groups of martyrs (6:9–11; 12:11; 17:6) and to "war" against the saints who follow Jesus (12:17; 13:7). We recall that John finds himself on Patmos "on account of the word of God and the testimony of Jesus" (1:9).

Historians cannot document a major outbreak of persecution against Christians in Roman Asia during the first century (Moss 2013). Chances are the seven churches were experiencing pressure on account of their faith, pressure that had escalated to a deadly level in at least one instance. We'll explore *why* they may have felt such pressure shortly.

The letters also indicate trouble with the churches' Jewish neighbors. The language is ugly: John calls them "those who say they are Jews and are not—but are a synagogue of Satan" (2:9; see 3:9). No easy explanation excuses such language, especially since Jews have endured centuries of persecution at the hands of Christians. However, understanding Revelation requires that we look into these troubling passages.

Because John accuses the Jews of slander (2:9), many historians have developed a likely explanation. (Not all agree.) Revelation was written before "Judaism" and "Christianity" had developed into separate world religions. Many "Christians" were also "Jews" just as James, Peter, and Paul had been Jews. John, like many in his audience, probably belonged among this group. It seems likely that the presence of Jesus followers threatened the stability of the synagogue, perhaps because the confession of a crucified messiah smacked of political subversion. It also seems likely that synagogue members simply pointed out that the Jesus people did not represent the rest of the group. At any rate, the letters suggest that a painful rupture divided the churches from the neighboring synagogues.

Threatened by persecution from their pagan neighbors and in hostile relations with the synagogues, these little churches also experienced internal tensions. The letters indicate several conflicts with competing Christian leaders. The monikers Balaam, Jezebel, and Nicolaitans reflect not their real names but hostile epithets. Balaam is the infamous prophet who led Israel into idolatry (Numbers 22–24), and Jezebel (1 Kings 16–21; 2 Kings 9) is the wife of King Ahab, who promoted worship of the deity Baal within Israel. The term Nicolaitans is new to us, but its root meaning (people conquerors) is very much like that of Balaam (lord of the people).

Revelation accuses these competing leaders of promoting idol-food and sexual immorality. Perhaps these prophets condoned literal promiscuity, but few interpreters think so. Instead, it appears that John is drawing upon the common biblical tradition that spoke of religious infidelity in terms of sexual promiscuity. In other words, it seems that Revelation accuses competing Christian leaders of promoting idolatry.

Idolatry as Promiscuity

Some Hebrew prophets employed promiscuity as a metaphor for religious idolatry. The book of Hosea provides the most striking example. At the beginning of the book, Hosea receives this commission:

> When the LORD first spoke through Hosea, the LORD said to Hosea, "Go, take for yourself a wife of whoredom and have children of whoredom, for the land commits great whoredom by forsaking the LORD." (1:2)

The remainder of Hosea continues to draw upon the prophet's relationship with his wife Gomer as a means to discuss Yahweh's relationship with Israel.

> Do not rejoice, O Israel! Do not exult as other nations do; for you have played the whore, departing from your God. You have loved a prostitute's pay on all threshing floors. (9:1)

Other prophets, notably Ezekiel and Nahum, used this same metaphor. We will encounter this phenomenon again in session six.

It is helpful to remember that the Nicolaitans, Balaam, and Jezebel are *Christian* leaders. John considers them false prophets, but a historian would consider them competing Christians. They worship Jesus, and they have followers among the churches. There must have been *reasons* other Christians followed them. But John regards his disagreement with them in absolute terms. These leaders and their followers have stepped outside the acceptable boundaries of discipleship and stand under judgment.

This conflict may lead us to understand *why* early Christians were experiencing pressure. The Asian cities were extremely religious, such that religion permeated everyday life. We recall the enthusiasm Ephesus expressed to the goddess Artemis from Acts 19 and the shrine to Asclepius outside Pergamum. Good citizens demonstrated their loyalty by offering worship toward Rome. Every household had its household gods. Perhaps even more important, social groups like trade guilds and burial societies had their own patron deities. Every public event, including meals, featured sacrifices and prayers to the appropriate deities.

Thus, the problem. Any Christian who wanted to do business or advance in society would be confronted with it on a regular basis: Do I participate in this party, banquet, meeting, or festival, or do I withdraw out of my exclusive devotion to Jesus? How Christians addressed these challenges could directly affect their income, their status, and their relationships. John's opponents advocated compromise. After all, those gods aren't real: what harm is there, for example, in attending the stone masons' banquet? But John demands absolute purity, keeping one's garments sparkling white (3:4).

Christians throughout the ages have faced the tension between loyalty to Christ and getting along within the broader culture. During the days of segregation some Southern Christians developed interracial communities, but most white Christians promoted, or at least tolerated, racial injustice. The segregation code was enforced both by low-level social pressure and by the threat of violence. Some Christians leave their jobs when they face exploitative business practices, but many prefer not to rock the boat. And some Christians tend to equate their political agenda with faithfulness to the gospel. We may not face the exact same challenges the seven churches encountered, but each age carries its own tests of faithfulness.

FOR FURTHER STUDY AND REFLECTION

Meditate

1. Read Revelation 3:15–16 three times (aloud if you're able), noting your emotional response to this passage.

Research

1. Professor Craig Koester of Luther Seminary in Minnesota is a leading interpreter of Revelation. Check out his presentations and interviews about Revelation and the seven cities that are posted online at www.enterthebible.org.

2. Review the stories of Balaam (Numbers 22–24), Jezebel (1 Kings 16–21; 2 Kings 9), or both. How do these stories help you understand what John is saying about his competitors?

Reflection

1. Reflect on your weekly schedule. Apart from church, how many events include prayers, sacred readings, and other religious expressions? Do you belong to any groups in which these religious expressions cause you discomfort?

2. Some Christian missionaries require new converts to cut all ties to their religious heritage. This poses a problem in societies like Burma/Myanmar and Cambodia, where traditional religious practices shape daily life to a high degree. Some converts must choose between their new faith and their families. In contexts like these, would you tend to recommend compromise or absolute purity?

3. The letters to the churches include distinct modes of address, from comfort to admonition to exhortation. Some letters combine these features. If you were writing a letter to Christians in your city, what tone would you take? What concerns would you emphasize?

4. When have you felt tension between faithfulness to Christ and getting along with your neighbors?

3 | "WHO IS WORTHY?"

Authority and Worship

SUMMARY

Three themes weave themselves throughout Revelation: authority, worship, and loyalty. Revelation depicts a fundamental conflict between Jesus Christ and the forces of evil. In this conflict, people demonstrate loyalty and offer worship to one authority or the other. But what kind of authority do we encounter in Jesus Christ? Revelation's most dramatic scene promises the "Lion of Judah" who can open the scroll of destiny. Instead of a Lion, however, John sees a Lamb. Though surely fearsome, Jesus Christ reigns not through Lion power but with Lamb power.

BASIC BIBLE REFERENCES

Revelation 4–5

WORD LIST

Cosmology
Anthropomorphism

3

"WHO IS WORTHY?"
Authority and Worship

People have diverse tastes in worship, and churches seem happy to oblige. Some go for "smells and bells," the kind of worship that communicates to everyone that something special is going on. Priests wear dazzling vestments. Altars shimmer with candlelight. Stained glass windows recount the mysteries of the faith. Kneeling and reciting, singing songs unlike any others they know, ordinary worshipers behave in ways they never behave anywhere else. Contrasting with such "high church" experiences, "free church" worship resembles nothing so much as a low-key pop music concert. People dress casually, and that includes the worship leaders. The preachers tell jokes and entertaining stories, and the music sounds little different than what folks listen to as they drive to work in the morning. While one church constantly reminds us of the difference between God's world and our ordinary lives, another church seeks to "meet people where they are."

How we worship tells us a great deal about what we value. In a college Introduction to Religious Studies class, students were required to write field reports from visits to local worship services. The students were expected to observe worship in traditions very different from their own. One student had been raised in a Baptist congregation that did not even print a worship bulletin. Having visited a Roman Catholic church, this student described "their so-called prayers." The prayers in his church had always been extemporaneous, unscripted, so he assumed that all true prayer must "come from the heart." Having been deeply formed in the tradition of his own congregation, this student could not imagine how scripted prayers might also express authentic spirituality.

Worship Scenes

If Revelation is "about" anything, it is about worship. The book identifies itself as a "revelation of Jesus Christ," and it often reveals Jesus in the very context of worship. "I was in the Spirit on the Lord's day," John tells us, when he first encountered the risen Jesus (1:10) and received the letters to the seven churches. He does not see Jesus again until the passage for this session (5:1–14), where Jesus receives worship in the heavenly throne room. The language of worship appears in most of Revelation's twenty-two chapters. Heavenly throngs sing to Jesus (14:3; 15:3–4) just as they sing to God (4:8).

Revelation 4:1 marks a major turning point in the book as a whole, and it opens the way to John's encounter with Jesus in chapter 5. John describes the crucial moment this way:

> After this I looked, and there in heaven a door stood open! And the first voice, which I had heard speaking to me like a trumpet, said, "Come up here, and I will show you what must take place after this."

Again, John finds himself "in the Spirit," as he did in Revelation 1:10, and now he stands in the heavenly throne room. The scene evokes Isaiah 6, where the prophet writes, "I saw the Lord, sitting on a throne" (Isaiah 6:1). There, heavenly beings proclaim:

> Holy, holy, holy is the LORD of hosts; the whole earth is full of his glory. (Isaiah 6:3)

In Revelation 4, John hears a different set of heavenly beings proclaiming God's praise:

> Holy, holy, holy, the Lord God the Almighty, who was and is and is to come. (Revelation 4:8)

36

Few people realize that the Hallelujah Chorus in Handel's *Messiah* derives from two passages in Revelation, 19:6 and 11:15. The *Messiah* concludes with Revelation 5:12–13, taken from the passage we are considering at the moment.

John continues to observe events from his heavenly outpost throughout the rest of Revelation, but the specific focus remains with the heavenly throne throughout chapters 4–6.

Revelation's emphasis on heavenly worship has heavily influenced Christian liturgy and art through the centuries. Arthur Wainwright notes that Revelation does not appear in the liturgies of the Eastern Churches. On the other hand, the most powerful Eastern icon features an image from Revelation 1:8—Jesus the *Pantocrator*, or Ruler-of-All. Meanwhile, Western liturgies often adapt Revelation's hymns of praise, including its descriptions of the New Jerusalem and the exalted Christ (Wainwright 1993, 212). Images from Revelation dot the church's hymnbooks, and they have inspired great artists such as Albrecht Dürer and William Blake.

Revelation also exerts great influence on the church's singing. Several hymns draw from Revelation 4–5, where John observes the heavenly throne. These include prominent hymns such as "Come, We That Love the Lord," "God Himself Is with Us," "Ye Servants of God, Your Master Proclaim," "What Wondrous Love Is This," and of course, "Holy, Holy, Holy."

Throne Visions

Before we move to John's encounter with Jesus in chapter 5, we might pause and reflect upon the significance of such throne visions. The Jewish and Christian literary apocalypses frequently turn to Isaiah 6 and describe God's heavenly dwelling place. It's common for them to depict multiple layers of heaven—three, five, seven, or even ten heavens. Paul himself refers to an apocalyptic vision in which he enters the third heaven (2 Corinthians 12:2). We encounter this motif in apocalypses such as *2 Baruch* and the *Ascension of Isaiah*, as we do in the book of Daniel (7:9). The Gospel of Matthew, alone among the Gospels, records Jesus as referring to God's throne (5:34; 23:22; 25:31).

We modern people might be tempted to dismiss accounts of the heavenly throne as figments of ancient *cosmology*, the primitive ways in which ancient people imagined the world. Surely few today believe heaven has layers. Even though our confession of the Apostles' Creed describes Christ as being "seated at the right hand" of God, not many of us imagine Christ literally sitting next to the divine throne for all eternity. But before we dismiss this image too readily, we might consider its significance for John and his audience.

When ancient Jews and Christians portrayed God as sitting on a throne, they were engaging in *anthropomorphism*; that is, they were using human images to communicate something about God. But they were also making a claim about worship and power—a critical point for understanding Revelation. Human rulers, like the Roman emperor, did sit on thrones. Like the Lincoln Memorial, divine throne rooms aimed at once to inspire and to intimidate. Moreover, anyone who walked down the narrow main street in Ephesus, Pergamum, or any of the other Asian cities would find herself surrounded by temples to Rome and its emperors—also designed to inspire and intimidate. By portraying God as sitting on a heavenly throne, Revelation makes a claim about true power and authority: they come not from Rome but from God.

Revealing the ~~Lion~~ Lamb

Power and authority provide the driving concerns for Revelation 5:1–14. Chapter 4 closes with God receiving praise, but in chapter 5 a problem emerges. The One on the throne holds a scroll, and the scroll is sealed with seven seals. Who, in all creation, is worthy? Who possesses the authority to open the seals and unroll the mysteries of the cosmos?

Suspense builds. No one—no one in heaven, on earth, or under the earth—is qualified to open the scroll. John weeps bitterly—"greatly," in the Greek. Then he hears. One is worthy to open the scroll and its seals. The Lion of Judah, the Root of David, can perform this task.

More suspense. And this suspense provides a key to understanding Revelation, particularly Revelation's interpretation of power and authority. John awaits the Lion's appearance. The churches are in a rough spot. Although John describes the churches as a "kingdom, priests serving [Christ's] God and Father" (1:6), these same churches remain subject to persecution (1:9; 2:9–10, 13). John may reside on Patmos as a result of exile, and one believer, Antipas, has already died. Who really directs the world's destiny, particularly the plight of these vulnerable believers? The Lion of Judah, David's Root, evokes all of Israel's hopes for deliverance. This is the language of messianic hope, a fierce lion who will drive away Israel's enemies and install a new reign on earth. Suspense builds as John awaits the Lion's arrival.

But no Lion arrives. Not in this scene, not anywhere else in Revelation. No Lion arrives. In the Lion's place John sees a Lamb, "standing, as if it had been slaughtered" (5:6). Where John expects a Lion, there stands a wounded yet living Lamb. Indeed, throughout the rest of Revelation, the Lamb provides the primary symbol for Jesus Christ. In this vision, Lion power has been displaced by Lamb power.

In John's day, everyone knew how power worked. "Who is like the beast, and who can fight against it?" confess the world's inhabitants (13:4). Like all empires, Rome governed through the threat of violence—often backed by brutal suppression. Jesus himself had provided one such victim of Roman violence. Now John sees the risen Jesus standing, "as if [he] had been slaughtered" (5:6). But here the Lamb holds power and authority: he stands before the throne, and he receives the book and its seven seals.

The portrayal of Jesus as a lamb occurs only in a few locations within the New Testament. Paul identifies Jesus as the "paschal [or

Passover] lamb" (1 Corinthians 5:7). Acts compares Jesus to the slaughtered lamb of Isaiah 53:7. And 1 Peter speaks to how Jesus, like a perfect lamb, redeems his followers (1 Peter 1:19). Most notably, John's Gospel presents Jesus as the "Lamb of God who takes away the sin of the world" (1:29). The Gospel of John is the only one that describes Jesus's death as occurring on the day of Passover.

Lamb imagery draws upon Jesus's innocence and vulnerability. The apostle Paul reminds us, however, that in God's value system vulnerability does not imply powerlessness. Jesus's crucifixion, Paul says, should look like an embarrassment—literally, a *scandal*—according to ordinary logic, but it expresses the very power of God (1 Corinthians 1:21–25). The Roman authorities who crucified Jesus regarded him as an upstart, a potential threat to public order but a person of no particular worth. "None of the rulers of this age understood" how God's wisdom works; otherwise, "they would not have crucified the Lord of glory" (1 Corinthians 2:8).

Lamb power, not Lion power. John's vision of the heavenly throne room challenged the seven churches to recalibrate their assumptions about power. In Revelation 5, God rules not by violence but through Jesus's faithful witness.

Power, Fate, and Books

The suspense involving the ~~Lion~~ Lamb in Revelation 5 revolves around a book, specifically a scroll that is sealed with seven seals. When Revelation was written, nearly all books appeared not with covers and spines but as scrolls. "Who is worthy to open the scroll and break its seals?", asks the mighty angel (5:2).

At this point in Revelation, no one knows what to expect from this scroll. But Revelation draws much of its language and imagery from the books of Daniel and Ezekiel (Boxall 2006, 95). Ezekiel receives a scroll with writing on the front and the back like the scroll in Revelation: "Written on it were words of lamentation and mourning and woe"

(2:10). Daniel likewise mentions a book "that will help you understand what is to happen to your people at the end of days" (10:14, 21).

As we continue through Revelation, we realize that the Lamb's book has much in common with the books we encounter in Daniel and Ezekiel. Other apocalypses such as *1 Enoch* also locate end-time mysteries in books (Boxall 2006, 95). As the Lamb opens each of the scroll's seven seals, the world's fate opens up before us. Only the Lamb is worthy to reveal fate.

Ancient people devoted enormous attention to the question of Fate. I capitalize Fate because people so revered Fate, they worshipped it as a goddess, *Tyche*. Entire philosophical systems addressed the question of Fate. Stoics disciplined themselves to face any circumstance they might encounter. Epicureans sought to maximize pleasure and avoid pain by enjoying things in moderation. Cynics tried to escape attachment to property, family, status, and even health. All these movements prepared people for an uncertain future.

Consider the fragility of life in an ancient city. Average life expectancies for males hovered around forty and were more like 25–30 for females. Epidemics, infections, violence, pregnancy and childbirth, fires, and a host of other dangers could end life all too suddenly. The first-century Roman Empire was wracked by disastrous civil wars. It was natural, then, that people should worry about Fate.

Books played a peculiar role in the relationship between Fate and public life. Greeks and Romans alike revered holy places, from which priestesses known as Sibyls would pronounce profound riddles that encoded future events. The Roman Senate regularly consulted a collection of Sibylline Oracles until they were destroyed by fire in 83 BCE. Over a period of several centuries Jews and Christians alike produced volumes of their own Sibylline Oracles that interpreted the present and predicted future events.

The Lamb's ability to open the scroll provides a commentary on power and Fate. Only God, "the one seated on the throne," holds the scroll. And only the Lamb is worthy to open it. Despite their pretensions, no other powers, not even Rome and its emperor, stand worthy to manage the future.

Worship and Power

American Christians today face our own challenges. Just sixty years ago, churches lived by means of power and prestige. "Everybody" went to church. Today, on a typical Sunday in the United States only about twenty percent or so of Americans attend church. Magnificent church buildings stand in dilapidation, denominational offices face staff reductions, and the church's institutional power stands at a relative low. This decline generally holds true regardless of theology, worship style, ethnicity, or denominational identity. People don't go to church like they used to, and they no longer go to church because they feel obligated. Maybe it's time to evaluate what we really believe about worship.

For John, the Lamb's appearance provokes worship.

> You are worthy to take the scroll and to open its seals, for you were slaughtered and by your blood you ransomed for God saints from every tribe and language and people and nation; you have made them to be a kingdom and priests serving our God, and they will reign on earth. (Revelation 5:9–10)

> Worthy is the Lamb that was slaughtered to receive power and wealth and wisdom and might and honor and glory and blessing! (5:12)

> To the one seated on the throne and to the Lamb be blessing and honor and glory and might forever and ever! (5:13)

In session five we'll encounter another of Revelation's great symbols, the Beast. Like the Lamb, the Beast receives worship. According to Revelation, "the whole earth" offers worship to the Dragon (Satan, 12:9) and to the Beast (13:3–4). The Beast *compels* worship through its power and arrogance, but the Lamb elicits worship because it is *worthy*, having given its life to ransom saints "from every tribe and language and people and nation" (5:9).

The Lamb is not powerless, but its power works differently than ordinary power does. For one thing, the Lamb has submitted itself to death. Even as it stands it bears its wounds. Yet the Lamb has seven horns and seven eyes (5:6). In apocalyptic literature horns connote power, while eyes indicate knowledge or awareness. The Lamb may be vulnerable, but by no means is it weak (Yeatts 2003, 111).

Worship matters. When we worship, we demonstrate—for our own benefit and for the world's—what we truly value. In the spirit of Revelation 5, our worship also confesses what we believe about power and authority. Do we worship the Beast because of its power to accrue wealth and to kill, or do we worship the Lamb because of its faithful testimony? What do we really believe?

FOR FURTHER STUDY AND REFLECTION

Meditate

1. Read Revelation 5:12–13 three times slowly (aloud if you're able). How would you sing your praise to God and to the Lamb?

Research

1. Does your church hymnal include an index of scripture references? Find out which hymns reflect heavy influence from Revelation. What parts of Revelation are most popular among the hymns?

2. Read Martin Luther King, Jr.'s "Letter from Birmingham Jail." You can find it online. The Civil Rights Movement practiced non-violence, but it was hardly passive. How did King balance Lamb power with Lion power?

Reflection

1. Has your congregation discussed its form of worship? Why do you worship as you do? In what ways does the conversation reflect people's tastes and preferences, and in what ways does it reflect theological values?

2. What secular activities reflect traces of worship? Discuss how we bring worship into our social, entertainment, business, and political lives.

3. How does the worship life of your congregation communicate its values? What would an outsider learn about your congregation by visiting one of its worship services?

4. Discuss: Do you believe in Lamb power? Can you think of examples in which Christians have chosen, rightly or wrongly, between Lamb power and Lion power?

4 | Two Witnesses and a Woman in Distress

SUMMARY

In Revelation 11, two witnesses preach the truth in the holy city. Their faithful testimony ends when for the first time we encounter the Beast, who overcomes and kills them. Chapter 12 introduces us to the Woman Clothed with the Sun and the great Dragon who persecutes her even during her labor pains. Both conflicts reflect a combination of persecution and divine deliverance. God raises the two witnesses to heaven and delivers the woman. The Dragon continues to rage, but God's faithful ones overcome the Dragon through the "word of their testimony" (12:11).

BASIC BIBLE REFERENCES

Revelation 11–12

WORD LIST

Woman Clothed with the Sun
Dragon
Beast
Inhabitants of the Earth
Antiochus IV Epiphanes
Maccabean Revolt

4

TWO WITNESSES AND
A WOMAN IN DISTRESS

Readers who assume that Revelation is too confusing to understand can find all the evidence they need in chapters 11 and 12.

Here we meet two "Witnesses," but their identity is far from clear. Their powers remind us of Elijah, who could "shut the sky" (Revelation 11:6; 1 Kings 17:1), and Moses, who turned water into blood (Exodus 7:17–24). Are we to conclude that Revelation predicts the literal return of Moses and Elijah to preach the gospel, or is something else going on?

The two Witnesses testify in a city, identified as both the "holy city" and the "great city." Unfortunately, these references seem to point in two different directions, one to Jerusalem and one to Rome. For example, the reference to Gentiles trampling the temple grounds for forty-two months sounds a lot like Daniel's description of Jerusalem's plight (Daniel 7:25; 12:6–7). The city's association with Jesus's crucifixion (Revelation 11:8) also suggests Jerusalem. But Revelation is pointing to Rome when it speaks of the "great city" with code names like "Sodom and Egypt" (11:8) and "Babylon" (16:19–19:5).

After the martyrdom of the two Witnesses, in chapter 12 we meet the Woman Clothed with the Sun, who flees from the Dragon and gives birth to a son. Again, Revelation does not identify the woman or the child—but it does identify the Dragon as Satan (12:9). Interpreters generally identify Jesus the Messiah as the child who is

> ### *Citizen Kane* and Revelation: Challenging Symbols
>
> We often find ourselves trying to "decode" Revelation's symbols, as if every symbol points to one and only one reality. That may be the case in some instances: we have already seen how Revelation uses the image of a Lamb to portray Jesus.
>
> But symbols do not always point to one and only one reality. Like the infamous "Rosebud" in the great movie *Citizen Kane* (1941), a symbol can create a whole field of meaning. In *Citizen Kane,* Rosebud refers directly to the brand name of a snow sled—but it also evokes the warm associations of a lost childhood.
>
> We may never achieve certain identifications for all of Revelation's symbols, but that doesn't prevent those symbols from being meaningful.

born, but the Woman's identity remains disputed. Are we to understand her as Israel, from which the Messiah emerges; as Mary, the mother of Jesus; or more generically as the people of God?

Common Motifs

It may be possible to move forward without resolving the identities of the two Witnesses, the Holy City, and the Woman Clothed with the Sun. Such puzzles are interesting, and we would very much like a solid grasp on their meaning. Yet even without solving those puzzles, readers are left with lots to chew on.

At first glance it is unclear how the stories of the Witnesses and the Woman relate to one another. Only later do we learn that the Dragon and the Beast are in cahoots. The Beast derives its authority from the Dragon (13:4). At this point in Revelation, however, their relationship remains a mystery.

Nevertheless, the two major symbols in Revelation 11 and 12, the Witnesses and the Woman, share some things in common. For one thing, supernatural enemies stage a mortal threat against the Witnesses and the Woman. Not only do the Witnesses spew judgment against unnamed enemies (11:5–6)—they also confront the Beast, who makes war against them, conquers them, and kills them (11:7). As for the Woman, as soon as we find that she is giving birth, the great red Dragon appears in heaven, desiring to devour her newborn child (12:3–4). Even after it has been thrown down from heaven, the malicious Dragon pursues the Woman and her child (12:13–17).

Despite the threats against the Witnesses and the Woman, divine judgment vindicates their cause, while supernatural protection sees to their ultimate deliverance. During their careers, the Witnesses pronounce curses against their enemies: "fire pours from their mouth and consumes their foes" (11:5). After their deaths their enemies watch them ascend to heaven, then a great earthquake decimates a tenth of the city (11:11–13). As for the Woman, Michael and his angels engage the Dragon in combat and drive him down to the earth (12:7–9). When the Dragon pursues the Woman upon the earth, the earth protects her (12:13–17).

The Witnesses and the Woman face mortal threats. Supernatural adversaries oppose them. However, divine judgment intervenes on their behalf.

Participation in Revelation

Readers may have a hard time identifying with the fearsome Two Witnesses or the Glorious Woman Clothed with the Sun. One of Revelation's most interesting features, however, involves how it applies similar language to Jesus, to John, to his followers, and to the readers.

For example, Revelation describes Jesus Christ as "the faithful witness" (1:5; see 3:14). As we have seen, Revelation employs the language of "witness" or "testimony" in a distinctive way to speak of those who die for their public confession. It applies the same language to Antipas, a member of the church at Pergamum who has apparently died for his testimony (2:13). The martyrs around God's throne have borne their testimony (6:9; 20:4), just as the two Witnesses of Revelation 11 do.

When John says he writes from Patmos "on account of the word of God and the testimony of Jesus" (1:9), he identifies himself with martyrs like Antipas and with Jesus. In fact, John begins the book by claiming that he himself has *testified* to the word of God and to the *testimony* of Jesus Christ (1:2). If Jesus is "faithful and true" (19:11), so is the testimony John receives from Jesus (22:6).

John also invites the audience to share this status. In Revelation 1:9, he calls himself "your brother and partner with you in the persecution and the kingdom and the endurance that are in Jesus" (my translation). In chapter 12, a heavenly voice announces that the "brethren" (translated "comrades" in the NRSV) have overcome the Dragon "by the blood of the Lamb and by the word of their testimony" (12:10–11), language that occurs again in 12:17 and 19:10.

The language of witness and testimony isn't the only way in which Revelation identifies its audience with John and with Jesus. Revelation begins by identifying John as Jesus's "servant" (literally *slave*; 1:1). The book extends the language of slavery to Moses (15:3) and the prophets (10:7; 11:18). By addressing them as slaves on several occasions, Revelation invites its audience to join this exalted company (7:3; 19:2, 5; 22:3, 6).

The idea that Christians can identify with Jesus through their faithful witness is not unique to Revelation. In Philippians, Paul describes having suffered for Jesus and even of sharing in Christ's sufferings (1:29; 3:10; see Romans 8:17; 2 Corinthians 1:5). And 1 Peter encourages believers to rejoice when they share Christ's sufferings (4:13). We can only imagine that early believers found great encouragement in believing that whatever they suffered as a result of their faith joined them with Jesus in such an intimate way.

Preservation and Resurrection

One thing clearly distinguishes the Witnesses from the Woman and her Child. The Woman receives absolute protection. She and her Child are not harmed. By contrast, the Witnesses endure the death of martyrs.

> **Faithful Witnesses**
>
> Revelation links believers to Jesus in remarkable ways. Jesus died as a "faithful witness" (1:5). So may believers who conquer by their testimony (12:11). Like Antipas, they too may qualify as "faithful witnesses" (2:13).

In their case, God restores them to life and takes them up to heaven (11:11–12).

Perhaps there's a lesson in this distinction between the Witnesses and the Woman—a lesson that may shed light on these two challenging symbols. As we have seen, many interpreters take the Woman to represent not an individual but a collective people: Israel or the people of God. Interpreters also identify the Witnesses as representatives of the saints, the followers of Jesus. However, the Witnesses may embody the martyrs as individuals.

If it is the case that the Witnesses represent God's people in some individual sense, while the Woman relates to God's people as a collective, their different fates begin to make more sense. Revelation promises faithful believers that they will "conquer" and find their names written in the Lamb's Book of Life. It does not promise believers that they will escape suffering and death. On the contrary, the path to ultimate salvation may pass directly through persecution.

> They have conquered him [the Dragon] by the blood of the Lamb and by the word of their testimony, for they did not cling to life even in the face of death. (12:11)

The symbol of the Woman testifies to another truth involving the people of God. As individuals "we are being killed all day long" for God's sake (Psalm 44:22), but God's work in the world will endure. As individuals we participate in that great people of God—a ministry God will see through to its ultimate fulfillment.

Persecution and Vindication

Both sets of images invite us to reflect on *the tension between persecution and vindication*. As soon as the two Witnesses begin their work, we hear: "If anyone wants to harm them, fire pours from their mouth and consumes their foes" (11:5). The Witnesses possess great authority: they can shut the sky, turn waters to blood, and strike the earth with plagues— but they seem to exercise these powers in response to persecution (11:6).

"The Inhabitants of the Earth"

In Revelation we encounter the phrase "the Inhabitants of the Earth" several times. Modern translations translate this phrase in different ways, including "those who dwell upon the earth." Revelation never defines this term, but it seems to apply to everyone who does not follow the Lamb. In other words, there are two classes of people: Followers of the Lamb and Inhabitants of the Earth.

Revelation's depiction of the Inhabitants is overwhelmingly sinister. They face enormous suffering and judgment, they persecute the Lamb's Followers, they worship the Beast, and they cavort with the Whore. In sessions seven and eight we will consider whether Revelation extends any hope towards the Inhabitants.

Indeed, opposition to the Witnesses comes from high places. Ultimately, the Beast conquers them, kills them, and leaves their bodies on display (11:7–8). This is our first encounter with the Beast, Revelation's symbolic embodiment of the great imperial forces that rebel against God and the Lamb. Indeed, our next session is devoted to the portrayal of the Beast in Revelation 13. For now, we simply note that the Witnesses give their lives for the sake of their testimony, a pattern we have already encountered in Revelation (1:5, 9; 2:13; 6:9–11).

Opposition to the Witnesses extends even beyond their death. "The Inhabitants of the Earth" celebrate their death. They do not allow the Witnesses' burial, and they gloat over their bodies. In other words, the whole world is set against the Witnesses and their activities.

Some contemporary believers, particularly in the United States, may struggle to imagine the context in which they might face resistance for their witness to the gospel. A few have lost jobs or relationships when they have stood up for ethical principles. Others have endured arrest or violence for standing up for justice, a tradition that reached a high-water mark in the Civil Rights and Black Lives Matter movements. But neither case is exactly the same as suffering simply for confessing allegiance to Jesus, a reality believers do experience in other parts of the world.

To appreciate Revelation's emphasis upon persecution and vindication, we have to dip into the cultural context in which the book was composed. We lack evidence of widespread official persecution of Christians during the first century. We do have lots of evidence from the Gospels, Acts, Paul's letters, and 1 Peter that Christians *anticipated* persecution and prepared for it.

At the same time, we should remember that Revelation is profoundly a Jewish book, very much engaged with the scriptures and concerns of Israel. Indeed, Jewish responses to persecution reached a high point during the very same period that saw the emergence of apocalyptic literature—and it is no coincidence. Books like Daniel—remember the fiery furnace and the lions' den?—provided encouragement for Jews who were risking their lives for their faith.

The books of 2 and 4 Maccabees deal with the Maccabean crisis and with the martyrdom of faithful Jews. Both books recount the story of a mother and her seven sons, who all suffer gruesome executions because they refuse to abandon God's law by eating pork. The mother encourages her seventh son:

Do not fear this butcher, but prove worthy of your brothers. Accept death, so that in God's mercy I may get you back again [in the resurrection] along with your brothers. (2 Maccabees 7:29)

Fourth Maccabees includes a remarkable statement—one that may sound familiar to Christians:

> These, then, who have been consecrated for the sake of God, are honored, not only with this honor, but also by the fact that because of them our enemies did not rule over our nation, the tyrant was punished, and the homeland purified—they having become, as it were, *a ransom for the sin of our nation.* And through the blood of those devout ones and their death as an atoning sacrifice, divine Providence preserved Israel that previously had been mistreated. (4 Maccabees 17:20–22; see Mark 10:45)

When John wrote Revelation, some Jews believed that God recognized the deaths of faithful martyrs, bringing salvation to God's people in recognition of their merit. Perhaps that idea lies in the background of Revelation 11–12.

Reflecting on Martyrdom

Few if any of us will likely face martyrdom. However, the martyrs have much to teach us. They can certainly correct the faulty preaching that we encounter in some churches.

Many preachers teach that Christianity is a path to happiness or success. Some preachers use the Bible to provide "practical" lessons for success in life—as if the Bible were a self-help manual full of nifty tips for marriage and business.

Revelation has a different point of view. According to Revelation, following the Lamb means going where the Lamb goes, even to the point of death (12:11). Revelation holds faithfulness as a greater value than happiness or success. Revelation sets before believers the proposition that the Lamb is "worthy" of our lives (5:9, 12).

Recent research in psychology suggests that happiness does not work well as an end in itself. Gaining wealth, enjoying good health, seeking exciting experiences, and having an active social life can all contribute to happiness—but only to a point. The true sources of happiness run deeper than that. They include making significant contributions to the world and participating in meaningful relationships, even when those commitments involve great sacrifice. (See the books by Haidt and Strawn, listed below.)

The strange visions of Revelation 11 and 12 challenge believers to ask, "What is worthy of my life?"

FOR FURTHER STUDY AND REFLECTION

Meditate

1. Read Revelation 12:11 three times, slowly (aloud if you're able). This verse, as much as any other, embodies the mindset John wants believers to share.

Research

1. Online or in a good Bible dictionary like the *Eerdmans Dictionary of the Bible*, the *HarperCollins Bible Dictionary*, the *Anchor Bible Dictionary*, or the *New Interpreter's Dictionary of the Bible*, look up Antiochus IV Epiphanes. He's likely to be listed among several figures named Antiochus. How might Antiochus's career affect how Jews and early Christians regarded imperial rulers?

2. A concordance is a tool that records every instance of a particular word in the Bible. Revelation 11:10 mentions the "inhabitants of the earth" (NRSV). Other translations render the phrase "those who live on the earth" (NIV), "those who dwell on the earth" (NASB), and so forth. Biblegateway.com provides an online resource for looking up key words. Go to biblegateway.com and select the New Revised Standard Version (NRSV): look up every occurrence of "inhabitants" in Revelation. How does Revelation depict the "inhabitants of the earth"?

Reflection

1. Let's reflect on the importance of symbols. Can you think of a symbol that has been significant to you and has a very clear meaning? Can you think of significant symbols from popular culture that open themselves to a wide range of meanings?

2. What do you believe are the major factors that contribute to happiness? Do you believe the gospel should contribute to happiness? In light of this study, how does the gospel relate to happiness?

3. What, in your opinion, can martyrs teach the church?

4. This study distinguishes between individual followers of Jesus, who may die for their faith, and the whole people of God, whom God will protect. Do you believe God protects Christians as individuals or as a group?

DRAGON AND BEAST

Revelation's Response to Empire and Power

SUMMARY

The great conflict between the Lamb's followers and the powers of
evil comes into full view in chapter 13, when Revelation reveals the
Beast and the Other Beast. Empowered by the Dragon—Satan—the
Beast demands loyalty and worship, persecuting the Lamb's followers.
This session explains how the Beast reflects Roman imperial domination, while the Other Beast points to those Asian citizens who promote
the imperial cult. The conflict regarding authority, worship, and loyalty
emerges especially clearly at this point in Revelation.

BASIC BIBLE REFERENCES

Revelation 13

WORD LIST

Bible prophecy movement
Augustus
Imperial cult
Pliny the Younger
Nero

DRAGON AND BEAST
Revelation's Response to Empire and Power

> *Then the dragon took his stand on the sand of the seashore. And I saw a beast rising out of the sea, having ten horns and seven heads; and on its horns were ten diadems, and on its heads were blasphemous names.* (Revelation 12:18–13:1)

In our public culture, the Beast has captured more attention than any other symbol in Revelation. Nutty Bible prophecy interpreters have worked tirelessly to unravel the Beast's number, 666 (13:18). For centuries, the Beast's associations with worship and with Rome (something more clearly revealed in Revelation 17) have led some Protestants to link the Beast to the Pope. Political figures and institutions have also commanded attention: a popular series of apocalyptic novels identifies the Beast as the general secretary of the United Nations, a common identification in today's Bible prophecy circles. Others have looked to technology: no one can buy or sell without the Beast's mark (13:17). In the 1980s, some folks linked the Beast to the bar codes attached to various consumer products. In short, people have responded to Revelation 13 by identifying the Beast with pretty much anything they find frightening or objectionable.

The Bible Prophecy Movement

Think 2050. According to a 2010 poll by the Pew Research Center, 41% of Americans believed Jesus "definitely" (23%) or "probably" (18%) would have returned to earth by the year 2050. Although slightly more Americans (46%) believed Jesus probably would *not* return by 2050, a strong 58% of white evangelicals did expect Jesus's return within forty years.

We all know polls can be misleading. In fact, pollsters routinely research popular end-time expectations, with the very results we'd expect: the numbers vary from one poll to another. But one thing remains stable: lots of Americans believe that Revelation predicts future events, and lots believe Jesus is coming soon.

Scholars refer to this phenomenon as the "Bible prophecy movement." Bible prophecy teachers say that the Bible, especially Revelation, provides a road map for the future. Many claim that today's news somehow fulfills the prophecies found in Revelation and other books. Bible prophecy teaching is common on television, the internet, and in publishing.

This approach to understanding Revelation isn't new, but its influence has certainly increased since 1960 or so. Perhaps this growth relates to the Cold War, when people were confronted by the reality

The Millerites

One famous manifestation of the Bible prophecy mindset occurred in 1843 and 1844. William Miller, an earnest believer in upstate New York, calculated Jesus's return for the period between March 21, 1843 and March 21, 1844. Miller published a book and went on a speaking tour, gathering thousands of followers, the "Millerites."

After March 21, 1844 passed, Miller saw the need to revise his calculations, finally settling on October 22, 1844. In anticipation of Jesus's return, some believers left crops in the fields, settled debts, and gave away their property. After the day passed his followers remembered it as the "Great Disappointment": "We wept, and wept, until the day dawn." Ever since the Millerite phenomenon, few prophecy teachers have dared to set actual dates for Jesus's return.

For more on the Millerites, see O'Leary 1994, 93–133.

that weapons we had created could end civilization as we know it. Over time, Bible prophecy teachers have moved from one fixation to another. From the Soviet Union to Middle Eastern oil crises, from Saddam Hussein to the emergence of China as a global power, from the European Union to global terrorism, prophecy teachers have credited Revelation with "predicting" one crisis after another.

Biblical scholars don't see it that way. In session one, we outlined why Revelation best makes sense when we interpret it in its own historical context. After all, Revelation was addressed to seven specific churches and the circumstances that confronted them. It speaks to the religious, political, and social circumstances of that time and place. Just as it is with Paul's letters and other biblical literature, contemporary Christians find Revelation meaningful by trying to understand when and why it was written (Rossing 2004).

The prophecy teachers distort the Bible in two particular ways. First, they use what I call a "Jigsaw Puzzle" approach to the Bible. They create complicated end-time systems by piecing together verses that are scattered throughout books like Daniel, Zechariah, Matthew, 1 Thessalonians, 2 Peter, and Revelation. This approach assumes that God has revealed the future by hiding secret messages in different parts of the Bible. (And it ignores what those passages mean in their own contexts.) When you stop and think about it, the Jigsaw Puzzle approach makes God look pretty silly, as if God were playing games with Bible readers.

We might call the second distortion the "Dick Tracy Apocalyptic Decoder Ring" approach. Bible prophecy teachers assume that Revelation's symbols point to contemporary historical phenomena. The problem is you can fit pretty much any symbol to anything you want. Do the scary locusts in Revelation 9 "predict" Cobra helicopters? Does Revelation 13:17, in which no one can buy or sell without the mark of the Beast, refer to modern systems of credit or inventory tracking?

With the Jigsaw Puzzle and the Apocalyptic Decoder Ring, it's no wonder prophecy teachers can link Revelation to just about any current event.

BEAST-LY

It is tempting to make fun, but the Beast is serious business. Empowered by the Dragon—Satan (12:9)—the Beast emerges from the sea. Its blasphemous names challenge the authority of God. "The whole earth" follows the Beast and worships it. As well they might, for "Who is like the beast, and who can fight against it?" (13:4).

The whole earth worships the Beast in wonder. Revelation's portrayal of the Beast reminds readers of Daniel 7, where a series of monsters persecutes God's people. By alluding to Daniel 7, Revelation encourages its readers to fear and resist the Beast.

A quick comparison of Revelation 13 with Daniel's vision reveals several remarkable commonalities. The beasts in Daniel and Revelation alike emerge from the sea. Daniel offers four beasts, including beasts that resemble a lion, a bear, and a leopard. Daniel leaves the fourth beast unnamed. Revelation presents a single beast, yet this beast bears the features of a leopard, a bear, and a lion—the same animals, but in reverse order. Daniel's fourth beast has ten horns; Revelation's single beast has ten horns. And while Daniel's fourth beast speaks "arrogantly," we soon learn that Revelation's Beast also speaks "haughty and blasphemous words" (Revelation 13:5). Indeed, the Greek text of Daniel uses the same word for "haughty," *megala* (meaning "great"), that Revelation does.

Descriptive Words

Take a few moments with pencil and paper, jotting down every bit of information Revelation 13 provides about the Beast. You might develop quite a long list.

... and four great beasts came up out of the sea, different from one another. The first was like a lion and had eagles' wings. Then, as I watched, its wings were plucked off, and it was lifted up from the ground and made to stand on two feet like a human being; and a human mind was given to it. Another beast appeared, a second one, that looked like a bear. It was raised up on one side, had three tusks in its mouth among its teeth and was told, "Arise, devour many bodies!" After this, as I watched, another appeared, like a leopard. The beast had four wings of a bird on its back and four heads; and dominion was given to it. After this I saw in the visions by night a fourth beast, terrifying and dreadful and exceedingly strong. It had great iron teeth and was devouring, breaking in pieces, and stamping what was left with its feet. It was different from all the beasts that preceded it, and it had ten horns. I was considering the horns, when another horn appeared, a little one coming up among them; to make room for it, three of the earlier horns were plucked up by the roots. There were eyes like human eyes in this horn, and a mouth speaking arrogantly. (Daniel 7:3–8)

And I saw a beast rising out of the sea, having ten horns and seven heads; and on its horns were ten diadems, and on its heads were blasphemous names. And the beast that I saw was like a leopard, its feet were like a bear's, and its mouth was like a lion's mouth. And the dragon gave it his power and his throne and great authority. (Revelation 13:1–2)

Something is going on here. Daniel was written in the midst of the Maccabean Crisis, when a local emperor, Antiochus IV, was oppressing faithful Jews. Daniel 7 reviews a series of great empires that had dominated Judea: the Babylonians, Medes, Persians, and finally the Greek empire of Alexander the Great. Antiochus inherited one segment of that great empire. Daniel 7 reminds its audience that God's people have survived a series of imperial oppressors. The current one will pass away just as the others did.

Revelation takes Daniel's imagery and does an amazing thing with it. Revelation's Beast takes the properties of all four of Daniel's beasts and rolls them all into one.

But what is Revelation trying to say? Like Daniel, Revelation is commenting on the empire of its day, Rome. According to Revelation, Roman imperialism poses a grim threat to believers, and it does so in several ways.

First, Rome tempts Jesus's followers to commit idolatry. Modern readers may find it difficult to believe, but worship of the emperor was extremely popular in Roman Asia at the time Revelation was composed. Around 9 CE the provincial council of Asia awarded a crown to its Roman proconsul, Paullus Fabius Maximus, for drafting the most eloquent honors to present to Augustus Caesar. The council determined to celebrate the birthday of "the most divine Caesar" as New Year's Day throughout the province. Their inscription, known as the Priene Inscription, identified the emperor Augustus as their "savior":

Craig Evans has provided a translation of the Priene inscription:

Since Providence, which has ordered all things and is deeply interested in our life, has set in most perfect order by giving us Augustus, whom she filled with virtue that he might benefit humankind, sending him as a savior, both for us and for our descendants, that he might end war and arrange all things, and since he, Caesar, by his appearance excelled even our anticipations, surpassing all previous benefactors, and not even leaving to posterity any hope of surpassing what he has done, and since the birthday of the god Augustus was the beginning of the good tidings for the world that came by reason of him, which Asia resolved in Smyrna.

(Evans 2000, 69)

"the birth of the god was the beginning of the good news [*evangelion*] through him."

A person who walked the streets of one of the great Asian cities would find herself surrounded by the trappings of imperial religion. The cities would compete for the privilege of hosting festivals in honor of the emperor, just as they would vie for the right to build temples in his honor. Ephesus alone hosted temples to the emperors Augustus and Domitian—and would later erect one to Hadrian (reigned 117–138 CE).

In session two, we saw that Rome did not impose its imperial cults upon the Asian cities; instead, local elites submitted bids to the Roman Senate for the rights to build temples and put on festivals. These demonstrations somewhat resembled modern cities competing for the Olympic Games, the Super Bowl, or a political convention. They showed off a city's importance, and they testified to its loyalty to Rome.

Revelation 13 reflects the reality that support from the imperial cults emerged from within Asia itself. In this chapter, the Beast comes from the sea, a standard way of describing foreign imperial oppressors in Jewish apocalypses (see Daniel 7:1–3). This first Beast rises *out of the sea* to utter blasphemous words and receive worship. But Revelation adds a *second* Beast that rises *out of the earth* (13:11–18). This second Beast promotes worship of the first, depicting local support for the imperial cults.

Second, the imperial cults challenged Christians' loyalty. The problem was not merely theoretical. Participation in the cults involved civic pride: people would notice if someone declined to participate. Historian Steven J. Friesen has shown that the imperial cults placed persons in literally hundreds of roles—with participation open to larger segments of society through "sacrifices, processions, concerts, mysteries, competitions, festivals, and so on" (Friesen 2001, 185). In other words, the imperial cults created a rallying point for the population, especially those upwardly mobile and aspiring persons who wanted to build social and business networks. Persons could sponsor and equip choirs, decorate public spaces, and provide other civic services—just as businesses today sponsor local parks and events.

Revelation poses the imperial cults as a direct challenge to loyalty. Naturally, Christian tradespeople and merchants would appreciate the opportunity to remind their neighbors of their civic commitment. For John, however, such participation amounts to idolatry. John recognizes the economic stakes that attend the imperial cults: the second Beast

> causes all, both small and great, both rich and poor, both free and slave, to be marked on the right hand or the forehead, so that no one can buy or sell who does not have the mark, that is, the name of the beast or the number of his name. (13:16–17)

Third, Revelation identifies the Beast as a cause of persecution for the saints. The Beast makes war on the saints and conquers them (13:7). As we have seen, Revelation frequently demonstrates its concern with persecution. John is on Patmos because of the word of God and the testimony of Jesus (1:9), possibly as an exile. A certain "faithful witness" (*martys*) named Antipas has been executed (2:13). Hosts of martyrs cry for vengeance under the heavenly altar (6:9–11).

Unfortunately, historians cannot document enduring official or systematic persecution among the Asian churches or anywhere else during the late first century—our only sources for this reality are the allusions to persecution in Christian texts. Outbreaks of local persecution occurred, but the Romans had no formal policy against Christians. However, a document from several decades later may illuminate the situation. During the years 111–113 CE, Pliny the Younger governed the Roman province of Bithynia, a province in central Turkey that bordered Roman Asia. Pliny wrote to the emperor Trajan regarding the presence of Christians in his province (Pliny, *Letters* 10.96–97).

Pliny was not looking to persecute Christians when he received anonymous accusations concerning them: indeed, he had no idea what to do with them. Pliny would interrogate the suspects, then offer them the chance to pray before an image of the emperor. If those Christians refused to do so, persisting even after being warned their lives were at stake, Pliny figured they deserved execution. After all, stubbornness has it limits! Pliny further observed that the presence of Christians had harmed public morale: after this wave of accusations, traffic in the temples and trade in sacrificial animals both rebounded.

> You can read Pliny's correspondence with Trajan online at https://www
> .pbs.org/wgbh/pages/frontline/shows/religion/maps/primary/pliny.html.

This is a controversial point among historians, but Pliny's letter may provide some context for understanding Revelation 13. Local elites owned high stakes in the imperial cults, and refusal to participate rendered one suspect. After all, why wouldn't any loyal citizen acknowledge the emperor's greatness? Pliny himself was unaware of persecutions in the past, but he knew that loyalty to the emperor was not subject to compromise.

Finally, nearly everyone who reads Revelation wonders about the number of the Beast: 666 (13:18). Revelation invites those who have wisdom to "count" this number, for it is the number of a person. Few interpreters have been willing to resist the temptation, assigning a host of often bizarre solutions. One suggestion has persuaded more scholars than others, however. One first century emperor, Nero, did persecute Christians in the city of Rome. Ancient people often assigned numerical values to the letters of the alphabet, and the Hebrew values of *Neron Caesar* add up to 666.

This solution accounts for two other puzzling problems. Some of our ancient manuscripts render the number as not 666 but 616. In

Hebrew, the final letter *n* (nun) often drops from the end of nouns. Its value is fifty; thus, *Nero Caesar* adds up to 616, *Neron Caesar* to 666. Moreover, some early Christian texts imagine Nero returning from the dead to persecute the church. We find this legend in the *Sibylline Oracles*, in the *Ascension of Isaiah*—and in Revelation. Revelation 13:3 mentions a "mortal wound [that] had been healed" (see 13:12; 17:8). Perhaps Revelation is saying that John's audience should remember just how deadly the Beast can be. Nero killed thousands of believers in Rome a few decades earlier (64 CE). Christians should always rest uneasy in the presence of the Beast.

FOR FURTHER STUDY AND REFLECTION

Meditation

1. Read Revelation 13:3b–4 three times, slowly (aloud if you're able). This passage expresses how the Beast amazes "the whole earth."

Research

1. Online or in a good Bible dictionary like the *Eerdmans Dictionary of the Bible*, the *HarperCollins Bible Dictionary*, the *Anchor Bible Dictionary*, or the *New Interpreter's Dictionary of the Bible*, look up Nero. How might Nero's shadow influence how Christians regarded Rome and pagan society in general?

2. Read Pliny's letter to Trajan and Trajan's reply on the website of PBS's show *Frontline*, "Letters of Pliny the Younger and the Emperor Trajan," translated by William Whiston. What do you learn about popular attitudes toward Christians in Bithynia? What do you learn about Christians?

Reflection

1. Ancient people did not separate church and state as do modern societies like the United States. Religion was a civic matter. In the light of Revelation 13, can you identify times—from your own experience or from history—when loyalty to Christ conflicted with loyalty to nation or culture?

2. Revelation 13:15–17 depicts a situation in which those who refuse to worship the Beast make themselves vulnerable to economic hardship and even martyrdom. Can you identify occasions when faithful people have exposed themselves to hardship for the sake of the gospel?

3. In your view, are there any circumstances in which Christians should compromise faithfulness to Christ in order to participate in society and its economy?

6 | "THE GREAT WHORE"

Revelation's Response to Empire and Culture

SUMMARY

Revelation introduces a second symbol of Roman imperialism, the Whore who rides the Beast. At her very introduction, we learn that the Whore, however glamorous she may appear on first sight, is doomed. Revelation introduces three fundamental reasons for the Whore's judgment: she and her allies wage war against the Lamb and his followers, she builds unholy alliances with the earth's rulers, and her network of commerce enriches some by exploiting others.

BASIC BIBLE REFERENCES

Revelation 17–18

WORD LIST

Babylon

"THE GREAT WHORE"
Revelation's Response to Empire and Culture

Revelation deploys two major images for Roman imperial culture, the Beast and the Whore. We do not need absolute precision in interpreting these symbols. Revelation's symbols do not always fit into neat compartments. But two factors may assist us in interpreting the Whore and her relationship to the Beast. First, we learn that the Whore rides the Beast (17:3), assuring us of their close relationship. And second, while the Beast receives worship for its power, combining brute force with idolatry, the Whore is identified in terms of her relationships, particularly commerce. We do not want to be rigid in making these distinctions. Nevertheless, if the Beast evokes Roman power and authority, the Whore speaks to the system of commerce and diplomacy that "rides upon" Roman power.

Gender Problems

Before we step into this text directly, let's be honest: many readers will recoil from the image of Rome as a prostitute. As well they should. We cannot defend this imagery or explain away its offense. The image originates among prophets like Hosea. According to the book of Hosea, God calls the prophet:

> Go, take for yourself a wife of whoredom and have children of whoredom, for the land commits great whoredom by forsaking the Lord. (Hosea 1:2)

Revelation's gender imagery has provoked serious concern among many commentators. "Good" women appear as mothers (Revelation 12) and brides (Revelation 21), while "bad" women are defined in terms of their promiscuity (Jezebel and the Whore). Revelation even includes a remarkable line about the followers of the Lamb who "have not defiled themselves with women" (14:4). Some interpreters acknowledge the problem but emphasize that these are just "stock" or conventional symbols Revelation uses to make a point. Others say these symbols render Revelation highly problematic for modern readers. *Where do **you** stand?*

We encounter similar imagery in Ezekiel and Nahum, among other prophetic books that use sexual promiscuity as a metaphor for idolatry (O'Brien 2008, 63–75). We have already met similar imagery in Revelation's description of Jezebel, who is accused of adultery for promoting sexual immorality (*porneia*) and the eating of food sacrificed to idols (Revelation 2:19–29). These biblical books, Revelation included, describe prostitution as if it were just a wicked moral choice—but as we all know, very few women simply "choose" lives of prostitution. Almost always women find themselves consigned to that life on the basis of poverty and abuse. In the ancient world most prostitutes were enslaved. While we recognize that John is using the metaphor as a means of communicating something about Rome's "promiscuous" relationships with power and commerce, we cannot justify such language in any context. As Tina Pippin writes, "why does

Roman Prostitution

Revelation characterizes the Whore as a "great city" (16:19; 17:18; 18:10–21). Adorned with jewels and fine fabric, she consorts with powerful men like kings and merchants. Revelation presents the image of a powerful, prosperous prostitute.

the demise of an empire have to be symbolized by a sexually abused and devoured woman?" (2012, 630).

The "Great City"

We do not ignore the offensiveness of John's image, but we also recognize the point John seems to be making. Something is wrong with the "Great City"—so what is it?

We first meet the "Great City" in 16:19, just a few verses before her formal introduction. The "great Babylon" receives "the wine-cup of the fury of [God's] wrath" (16:19). Babylon is doomed even before we meet her.

Nevertheless, chapter 17 commences the formal introduction: "Come, I will show you the judgment of the great whore . . ." Revelation presents this scene with an extra dash of dramatic flourish. If we heard it read aloud, the Whore's appearance would generate a visual image. Let's consider how Revelation introduces her appearance.

- First the angel announces her judgment. We also learn of her promiscuity—and that the Inhabitants of the Earth are drunk from the "wine of her fornication" (17:1–2).

- Her initial appearance, however, provides mixed messages. Yes, she rides a beast with blasphemous names. We know this Beast. But she is also adorned with purple and scarlet, bedecked with precious jewels, and she holds a golden cup (17:3–4), all marks of luxury.

- Things turn nasty. When we peer into that cup, it's filled not just with wine but with filth. After we hear her name, "Babylon" (see 16:19), things grow even worse: she's drinking the blood of Jesus's followers (17:4–6).

No wonder John writes, "When I saw her, I was greatly amazed." The passage pulls us back and forth from disgust to glamor and back

> ## Rome as Babylon
>
> Three Jewish apocalypses, all composed during roughly the same period as Revelation, also employ Babylon to characterize Rome. *Second* and *Third Baruch*, along with *Fourth Ezra*, all begin with a prophet's lament concerning Jerusalem's destruction by the Babylonians. (You can find 4 Ezra as chapters 3–14 in the apocryphal 2 Esdras.)
>
> As we continue to read, we realize that none of these apocalypses are really speaking to the sixth century BCE, when Jerusalem fell to Babylon. Instead, they're using Babylon's conquest as a literary setting in which to reflect on how Rome had devastated Jerusalem in 70 CE. These apocalypses share a common complaint: perhaps Jerusalem had provoked divine judgment, but "Are the deeds of those who inhabit Babylon any better? Is that why it has gained dominion over Zion?" (4 Ezra 3:28). In other words, why would God use a corrupt pagan empire to judge God's own people?

to disgust. And that is what an apocalypse does: things may present one appearance, but an apocalypse *reveals* their true significance. The woman may look glamorous, but in reality, she is drunken and murderous. Rome may generate enormous luxury—for some—but the discerning eye will see that the whole imperial system is corrupt and deadly.

Throughout this study of Revelation we have avoided over-simple and too-direct explanations for Revelation's symbols. However, this passage speaks to us more directly than most. The angel accompanying John even offers an explanation for this bizarre image. The woman rides a Beast, and the Beast's seven heads indicate seven mountains (17:9). In John's day, just as now, folks have known Rome as "the city on seven hills."

Now we know that the "Great City" teaches us something about Rome. But Revelation presents the Whore not as "Rome" but as "Babylon" (16:19; 17:5). This may seem odd to some readers, even unnecessary, but other Jewish literature after the year 70 CE also employs Babylon to speak of Rome. In the New Testament, 1 Peter 5:13 makes the same association. The Rome as Babylon link boils down to one reality: just as the Babylonians captured Jerusalem and destroyed its temple in 587 or 586 BCE, the Romans likewise conquered the city and decimated its temple in 70 CE.

Revelation 17:16 creates one of Revelation's most puzzling moments: the Beast comes to hate the Whore. It is not God who brings the Whore to destruction. Instead, the Beast and its ten horns (kings who conspire with the Beast, according to 17:12) strip the Whore naked, consume her flesh, and burn her. The same alliance of the Beast and the ten kings who will make war against the Lamb (17:14) now destroy the Great City.

How can it be that the very Beast once ridden by the Whore turns upon her and kills her? Once the Beast loses its conflict with the Lamb, the Beastly alliance turns on itself. John is saying something about empire—not just the Roman Empire but all empires. We might remember that Rome endured a series of brutal civil wars just after Nero's reign. Moreover, many people in the ancient world resented Rome for extracting wealth, resources, and even people (enslaved persons) from its territories. In the long run, Rome's arrogance, violence, and greed cannot sustain themselves. They will turn inward, devouring the very system that (for now) "rules over the kings of the earth" (17:18).

Taunt or Dirge?

Many commentators identify Revelation 18 as a sort of funeral dirge for Babylon/Rome (Yarbro Collins 1980). Others see the passage as more of a taunt, mocking those who mourn the Empire's demise.

I tend to see Revelation 18 as a taunt rather than a mournful dirge. The passage begins, "Fallen, fallen is Babylon the great!" (18:2), and it moves on to warn God's people to "Come out" from the doomed city (18:4), for "mighty is the Lord God who judges her" (18:8). We have lots to learn from those who lament the Great City's fate. Revelation 18:3 informs us that kings have drunk from the wrathful wine of her promiscuity, while merchants have grown rich by means of her wealth. Later, three groups weep and wail over the fallen city.

- Kings mourn because the city has provided them with luxury (18:9).

- Merchants, who once "gained wealth from her" (18:15), now weep "since no one buys their cargo anymore." And what cargo it is! "Gold, silver, jewels and pearls, fine linen, purple, silk and scarlet, all kinds of scented wood, all articles of ivory, all articles of costly wood, bronze, iron, and marble, cinnamon, spice, incense, myrrh, frankincense, wine, olive oil, choice flour and wheat, cattle and sheep, horses and chariots, slaves—and human lives" (18:12–13).

- Finally, representatives of the shipping industry mourn, for they too have grown rich from Babylon's wealth (18:17–19).

"What Have the Romans Done for Us?"

The Monty Python film *Life of Brian* dramatizes the divided loyalties Rome's subjects may have felt. The character Reg wants to start a revolution: "They've bled us white, the bastards. They've taken everything we had, and not just from us, from our fathers, and from our fathers' fathers."

Having incited the crowd, Reg makes a mistake. He asks, "And what have they given us in return?" Various voices chime in: "The aqueduct." "And the sanitation." "And the roads." "Irrigation." "Medicine." "Education." "And the wine."

The list makes the point. Revelation takes sides with those who despise Rome for its exploitative ways (not to mention its idolatry). But many in Revelation's audience might well have been grateful to Rome for stimulating the economy and providing order. That's how it is with empires: they simultaneously give and take away.

The songs in Revelation 18 mount a critique of how empires work. Diplomacy, the relationship between Rome and the earth's petty rulers, amounts to promiscuity. The empire generates enormous wealth for some—but only at the expense of human lives. Note how the cargo list in 18:12–13 enumerates one luxury item after another, then moves toward the implements of war (horses and chariots), and finally to the human cost of empire. Revelation's readers could not forget that about 16–20 percent of the Empire's population consisted of enslaved persons (Bartchy 2013, 170). Economic inequality defined life in the Roman world. Everyone knew how wide the gap was between those who possessed unimaginable wealth and the masses. As Allan Boesak put it, "The wealth of Roma Mater was built on the continuing exploitation of weaker nations, on the robbing of the colonies, and on slave labour" (1987, 110).

Revelation and Resistance

Within the New Testament canon, Revelation stands alone for its explicit critique of Rome—not only for its arrogance and idolatry (chapter 13), but also for its violent and exploitative ways. Throughout the centuries some readers have seen in Revelation a call to resist tyranny and oppression. The German Peasants' Revolt of 1524–1525 involved casualties mounting up to the six figures. The peasants demanded a dozen economic and social reforms, including lower rents and the restoration of public property. Thomas Müntzer, a primary leader of the revolt, understood Revelation as unveiling the arrival of God's kingdom on earth. Martin Luther, on the other hand, opposed the Revolt because it blended religious fanaticism with unchecked violence. Luther encouraged the authorities to "stab, smite, and slay" the rebels. Elsewhere he reflected, "It is pitiful that we have to be so cruel to the poor people, but what can we do?" (quoted in Smith 1914, 164).

But Revelation inspires more than fanaticism. One outstanding book on Revelation emerged from the pen of the black South African anti-Apartheid activist and pastor-theologian Allan Boesak. Held in solitary confinement and recalling the tradition of John's exile to Patmos, Boesak felt what he called an "angelic visitation" (1987, 9). A sense of peace and purpose came over him and pulled him through this difficult period. Boesak had been studying Revelation for several years. He describes his experience this way:

> Arrested, threatened, imprisoned in solitary confinement, walking into rifles and machine guns, tear-gassed in churches, faced with horrors I had never dreamed of, seeing our children die on the streets, watching South Africa becoming less and less our mother and more and more our grave.... During these years, I believe, I have discovered the heart of that lonely, brave prophet on his island.... For I know now what he knew then. Jesus Christ is Lord. (1987, 14)

Today, Revelation leads many serious interpreters to criticize the global economic and political networks, and often the role of the United States, for funneling wealth to a few people at the expense of masses (see Rhoads 2005). The judgment of Babylon challenges modern readers to assess how and whether contemporary "cities" bear significant resemblances to the "Great City."

FOR FURTHER STUDY AND REFLECTION

Meditate

1. Read Revelation 18:11–13 three times, slowly (aloud if you're able). These verses encapsulate Revelation's condemnation of Roman commerce.

Research

1. Has your denomination issued statements on economic policy? You can usually go online and search terms such as the *name of your denomination, globalization, economy, economic justice, taxation,* or *labor,* and find these official documents. How has your church spoken to economic justice?

2. Find a good Bible dictionary like the *New Interpreter's Dictionary of the Bible,* the *Anchor Bible Dictionary,* the *HarperCollins Bible Dictionary,* or the *Eerdmans Dictionary of the Bible,* and look up the essays on "slave," "slavery," or "trade and commerce." What findings seem significant to you?

Reflection

1. Review the discussion box, "What Have the Romans Done for Us?" If you were present in that conversation, would you defend the Romans or criticize them?

2. Most readers of this study guide will live in the United States or other affluent societies. How should Christians respond to the relative wealth, power, and privilege associated with living in nations like these? Do you regard Revelation 17–18 as relevant to this conversation?

3. Many readers express concern with Revelation's gender imagery, especially its depiction of female symbols such as Jezebel, the Woman Clothed with the Sun, Babylon, and the New Jerusalem. Could you imagine an alternative symbol for Rome's economic and diplomatic power? What would you suggest?

7 | COPING WITH JUDGMENT

SUMMARY

There's no denying it: Revelation features lots of judgment. In this session, we examine what judgment means in Revelation. We also reflect upon the biblical concept of God as judge. Modern Christians often recoil from God's role as judge; however, in a world in which judges routinely favored the rich and powerful, God's judgment sounded like good news to those who rarely tasted justice.

BASIC BIBLE REFERENCES

Revelation 19:11–20:15

WORD LIST

Judgment
Michael
Resurrection

7 | COPING WITH JUDGMENT

Few of us rest easy with the concept of judgment. Christians face the same challenge time and again. We recall Paul's instruction to "Examine everything," so that we may "hold fast to what is good" (1 Thessalonians 5:21). But when we feel compelled to speak out on a pressing issue of the day, someone is always ready to remind us, "Do not judge, so that you may not be judged" (Matthew 7:1). After all, a healthy dose of humility and introspection teaches us to be careful in assessing others. How would we fare if we were judged by our own standards? As we have seen, Revelation requires its audience to discern the world they inhabit and to choose one set of values over and against all other competing values. Few of us rest easy with that challenge.

Revelation 19:11–20:15 calls our attention to a different kind of judgment: final judgment. The chapter also raises some challenging problems. For example, why does the angel lock up the Devil, only to let Satan go free after a thousand years (20:1–2)? Are we comfortable imagining mortals, even righteous martyrs, receiving the reigns of judgment (20:4–6)? And how do we make sense of a resurrection that occurs in two stages, such as we encounter in this passage?

This study devotes one session to Revelation 19:11–20:15 and a separate session to Revelation 21–22. This division is somewhat artificial. Copyists added chapter and verse numbers to the biblical books centuries after John composed Revelation. In John's vision, everything

Biblical Judges

Modern Christians typically think of God's judgment as a fearsome thing—as well we should. As Hebrews 10:31 reminds us, "It is a fearful thing to fall into the hands of the living God." We all know our shortcomings, some of us more intensely than others, and none of us look forward to having them exposed or to facing their consequences.

As fearsome as judgment may seem to us, we might wonder why biblical audiences considered judgment a *good* thing. In prosperous modern societies, we associate judges with fair trials—but in the ancient world the masses of people stood among those who "hunger and thirst for justice" (a literal translation of Matthew 5:6). Throughout history most of the world's population has been like the persistent widow, who assumed that a judge would not grant her justice without an ulterior motive (Luke 18:2–8). This is why the Bible devotes a whole book to the judges God sends to deliver Israel. In contrast to ordinary judges, God provides true justice. What does judgment look like to an oppressed people?

from 19:11 through 22:21 might function as one unit. This longer section closes the book by announcing God's judgment upon the world and its powers and ushering in the vision of the new city God has in store. This session focuses upon the theme of judgment, while our final session will turn to renewal and hope.

War and Conquest

This session's segment marks a major turning point in Revelation. Revelation 4:1 transitions from Jesus's letters to the seven churches (chapters 2–3) as John sees a door open up in heaven. This transition moves us into the body of Revelation's vision, the things John sees from his heavenly point of view. Here again John sees heaven open up (19:11). Instead of a throne, John sees a rider on a white horse who "judges and makes war." We are now entering Revelation's final stage.

We have already encountered the language of making war in Revelation. The risen Jesus threatens to make war against wayward believers in the letter to the church in Pergamum (2:16). John describes a cosmic war between archangel Michael and his angels on one side and the Dragon and his angels on the other (12:7). Revelation also announces that the ten kings associated with the Beast will make war against the Lamb. The Lamb does not just conquer these opponents, but does so in part because of the faithfulness of his followers (17:14).

Revelation insists that its audience lives amidst grave conflict. Each of the letters to the seven churches extends its blessings "to the one who conquers," a promise reinforced by the affirmation that the Lamb's followers conquer because of the Lamb's powerful death and because of their faithful testimony (12:11; 15:2; 21:7). The dramatic throne scene in Revelation 5 includes the promise that the Lion can open the sealed book because he has conquered (5:5). Yet Revelation also recognizes that things do not work simply or easily. From time to time, the Beast and its allies seem to enjoy moments of conquest as well (11:7).

Many contemporary readers find the language of war and conquest repellant. Our history teaches us all too well the dangers that occur when people turn religion to violent ends. Not only wars between religions but wars among Christians escalate greatly when people believe their conflicts involve ultimate values and final truth.

Revelation pushes back against our resistance in at least two ways. First, we recall that in Revelation 5 the Lion never appears. Instead, we meet a Lamb who has endured and conquered death. Later on in this session we will explore the weapon this Lamb employs: a sword that protrudes from his mouth. Perhaps Revelation is not encouraging its audience to revel in violence but to consider the path of faithful, non-violent testimony.

But Revelation also confronts our discomfort with a challenge. Are we willing to consider the possibility that sometimes the gospel calls us to engage in conflict? Not necessarily violent conflict, but perhaps we face moments that call for decisive action. How do we discern when an issue is so serious that we cannot embrace compromise? In his "Letter from Birmingham Jail," Martin Luther King, Jr., confronted religious people who wanted to work things out diplomatically rather than embrace conflict. Violence was already present in the reality of racial oppression, King argued. Responsible people could not claim to live "above" conflict in that moment. Christians are indeed called to love, but authentic love sometimes requires acting for justice.

In the nineteenth century, America's largest Protestant denominations all split over the issue of slavery. Methodists and Presbyterians would not reunite until after the high moments of the Civil Rights Movement. Baptists still haven't reunited. Among Baptists, the division reached a crisis point over the question of foreign missionaries: should Christians send slave owners as missionaries?

We also recall the example of the German pastor and martyr Dietrich Bonhoeffer. Bonhoeffer firmly embraced pacifism. He believed that violence was always evil. Yet facing the atrocities of Hitler and his Nazi regime, Bonhoeffer participated in the German resistance. Most historians believe Bonhoeffer even participated in the plot to assassinate Hitler. Writing from prison, Bonhoeffer came to express the view that moral rules, even Christian moral rules, could not always provide the guidance Christians need. Sometimes believers simply must discern the most faithful course among morally impossible options. "In short," he wrote, "it is much easier to see a thing through from the point of view of abstract principle than from that of concrete responsibility" (1971, 7).

Revelation challenges us to embrace the possibility that some moments and some issues may force faithful people to take sides.

The Scenario

The passage begins with the heavens opening before John, revealing Jesus's dramatic appearance (19:11–16). The passage piles up descriptive phrases. Many of them remind us of other descriptions of Jesus scattered

The Thousand Years

Perhaps the most curious feature in Revelation 20 involves the thousand years in which Satan is bound—followed by Satan's release for one last spate of violence (20:7).

Through the centuries, countless interpreters have tried to fit these thousand years into a scheme of history. That approach is probably misguided. For example, Revelation 19:17–21 describes the defeat of massive armies, as does Revelation 20:7–10. We need not assume that Revelation is describing two very similar events at different points in time.

Perhaps Revelation's apocalyptic outlook regards evil as so pervasive that it cannot be eliminated in a single moment. One Jewish apocalypse envisions a 400-year messianic reign, followed by seven days of silence and then the resurrection and final judgment (2 Esdras 7:28–33). *First Enoch* also includes a two-stage judgment (10:4–6; see Isaiah 24:21–22; Aune 1998, 1078). We simply do not know why Revelation envisions two battles, two defeats of Satan, two resurrections, and two judgments.

throughout Revelation. For example, Revelation 3:14 calls Jesus the "faithful and true witness," just as 19:11 identifies Jesus as "Faithful and True." Jesus's eyes are "like a flame of fire," recalling his description in 1:14. We have already encountered the sword protruding from Jesus's mouth—twice (1:16; 2:16). Jesus is, after all, "King of kings and Lord of lords" (19:16).

Then comes the battle, so gruesome that an angel invites the birds to pick apart the bodies of the slain, people and horses, kings and captains, small and great (19:17–18). The Beast and the Other Beast meet their fate, thrown alive into the Lake of Fire (19:20). And the "rest," presumably masses of humanity, die at the edge of the rider's sword, with the birds gorging on their flesh (19:21).

In further developments we observe Satan's own judgment—in two stages, a thousand years apart. In a second battle, fire from heaven devours the nations that encamp against the saints (20:9). Finally, we observe a judgment before a great white throne. Books are opened, including the Book of Life that includes all the Lamb's followers (see 3:5; 13:8; 17:8). All those who do not appear in the Book of Life are thrown into a Lake of Fire (20:15).

Our passage also relates death's demise. Death and Hades return their dead. Moreover, the sea returns its dead (20:13–14). These images imply a bodily resurrection. Many people today imagine that when someone dies, their soul departs immediately to be with God. We often fantasize that our loved ones are watching down from heaven. That is not the case in Revelation—or in most of the New Testament. Revelation maintains that only the martyrs dwell in heaven (6:9–11), but it appears to assume that most people simply die and await the resurrection and the end of history. This is what Paul apparently believed (1 Thessalonians 4:13–18; 1 Corinthians 15:50–54).

The New Testament offers several different images concerning what lies beyond death. This is because the ideas of a final resurrection, a final judgment, and an afterlife were fairly recent and quite fluid in both ancient Judaism and earliest Christianity. Some people believed death was simply the end of life, a view reflected in passages that refer to Sheol as a murky place where God is not even named (see Psalm 6:5). In Jesus's day, the Sadducees held this view. (Remember their debate with Jesus concerning the resurrection? See Mark 12:18–28; Matthew 22:23–33; Luke 20:27–40). Paul talks about believers being "asleep" or dead before the resurrection, but Luke includes passages that suggest people meet their final destiny immediately upon death (Luke 16:19–31; 23:43).

Revelation certainly promotes belief in eternal life, but not in the romantic way we sometimes imagine. One of Revelation's most remarkable features is that at the end people do not rise up into heaven. Instead, the New Jerusalem descends to earth, where death no longer exists, nor do "mourning and crying and pain" (21:4).

Violence and Doom?

When we encounter the images of bloody conflict and fiery doom, modern readers often struggle with at least two questions. First, are we to imagine Jesus as violent? And second, does Revelation imagine that only a tiny number of saints will meet salvation while countless "Inhabitants of the Earth" face eternal torment?

These questions require some discipline on our part. We probably arrive at these questions with our opinions and values already well formed. Some of us may be comfortable with divine violence or the concept of hell, while others are not. We have to be willing to allow Revelation its own voice in the question, and we must be willing to acknowledge that what it says may not please us.

There's no denying the carnage depicted in Revelation 19 and no denying the Lake of Fire in chapter 20. Birds feast on flesh, while those whose names are not found in the Book of Life are "cast" into the fiery Lake. Moreover, if the Beast and the Other Beast suffer "day and night forever and ever" in the Lake (20:10), we cannot rule out that others face a similar fate. Many interpreters, however, understand Revelation to promote a peaceful Jesus, one who offers hope to all people rather than judgment for most and salvation for a few.

We deal first with Jesus. Jesus kills his enemies with the sword that protrudes from his mouth. Revelation could hardly be clearer about that (19:21). But are we to imagine that sword as a literal weapon? Several factors should make us wonder. For example, Revelation 19:11 introduces the rider as "Faithful and True," a title that recalls the description of Jesus as a "faithful and true witness" in Revelation 3:14 (see 1:5). We have already seen how Revelation celebrates "faithful witnesses" like Antipas, who suffered as martyrs (2:13; 12:11). We remember that Revelation 5 creates the anticipation that Jesus will appear as a great Lion, yet instead he stands as a Lamb that has been slaughtered (5:5–6). Could it be that Revelation transforms biblical traditions of

God's violent vengeance into a conquest that works through the Lamb's faithful testimony?

Military imagery appears here and there throughout Revelation—and not just because the Beast seems invincible: "Who is like the beast, and who can fight against it?" (13:4). Not only does Christ conquer his enemies (17:14), but each of the seven letters to the churches calls its audience to "conquer" as well. Revelation 21:7 blesses those who conquer, for "they will inherit these things," presumably life in the New Jerusalem. The 144,000 who follow the Lamb wherever he goes abstain from sex (14:4–5). Perhaps this detail reflects preparation for war along the lines of Deuteronomy 23:9–14. In any event, Revelation uses military language and envisions bloody conflict—but at no point does it encourage its audience to take up weapons and fight. The Lamb's followers conquer through their faithful testimony, not by taking up arms (12:11).

As for the Fiery Lake, things certainly look gloomy in chapters 19 and 20. Some readers, however, see more hopeful signs in chapters 21 and 22. For example, Revelation 21:3 depicts the New Jerusalem coming down from heaven so that God will dwell among mortals and "they will be [God's] peoples" (note the plural). After all, God is "making all things new" (21:5). Likewise, the new city's Tree of Life bears leaves that "are for the healing of the nations" (22:2). Does Revelation hold out hope for the Inhabitants of the Earth?

Many readers do advance optimistic, peaceful readings of Revelation, while others remain convinced that Revelation delights in the prospect of judgment. When Revelation describes the rider's robe as "dipped in blood" (19:13), we may hear echoes of Isaiah 63:3.

It is difficult to avoid the impression of grisly conflict and bloody judgment.

Some interpreters defend Revelation's violent visions. Revelation, some say, simply describes the world as it is. After all, Revelation was composed in a violent age, when Rome dominated other nations precisely through the threat of destruction and death. The Romans worshiped

ISAIAH 63:3	REVELATION 19:13–15
I have trodden the wine press alone, and from the peoples no one was with me; I trod them in my anger and trampled them in my wrath; their juice spattered on my garments, and stained all my robes.	He is clothed in a robe dipped in blood, and his name is called The Word of God. And the armies of heaven, wearing fine linen, white and pure, were following him on white horses. From his mouth comes a sharp sword with which to strike down the nations, and he will rule them with a rod of iron; he will tread the wine press of the fury of the wrath of God the Almighty.

Conquest, or Victory, in the person of the goddess *Victoria* (Latin) or *Nikē* (Greek, the very word Revelation uses for conquest). Violent regimes rarely pass away quietly. Other interpreters, like Allan Boesak, have argued that Revelation's violence is justified. Writing in the midst of South Africa's brutal Apartheid regime, Boesak said, "If [Christ's] cloak is spattered with blood, it is the blood of his enemies, the destroyers of the earth and of his children" (1987, 124).

The depictions of judgment in Revelation 19:11–20:15 tend to emphasize the doom that awaits the Lamb's enemies rather than the deliverance offered to his followers. Only a few moments single out the special hope extended to the saints. The martyrs inherit the first resurrection, where they join Christ in judging and reigning for a thousand years (20:4–6). We might remember that Revelation has already depicted the martyrs in heaven as they await vengeance (6:9–11). The depiction of the final judgment scarcely mentions the "Book of Life" and does not mention those whose names are included in it (20:12). The attention in this scene dwells upon the universality of judgment. All persons, "great and small," endure judgment "according to what they had done" (20:12–13). Revelation withholds its emphasis upon salvation for the book's closing vision.

FOR FURTHER STUDY AND REFLECTION

Meditate

1. Read Revelation 20:12 three times, slowly (aloud if you're able). This is Revelation's great judgment scene, and it has inspired countless works of art.

Research

1. What does your church teach regarding the afterlife? If your church has a book of worship, you might look up its funeral service, along with the creeds you recite in worship. What do these documents affirm about life beyond death? If you're really interested in the topic, you might read Jaime Clark-Soles, *Death and the Afterlife in the New Testament* (New York: T&T Clark, 2006); Dale B. Allison, *Night Comes: Death, Imagination, and the Last Things* (Grand Rapids: Eerdmans, 2016); or Greg Carey, *Eschatology* (Louisville: Westminster John Knox, 2022).

2. The themes of resurrection and judgment certainly play major roles in Revelation 19:11–20:15. Why not look up articles on resurrection, judgment, and Sheol in a good Bible dictionary (*New Interpreter's Dictionary of the Bible, Anchor Bible Dictionary, Eerdmans Dictionary of the Bible, HarperCollins Bible Dictionary*) and report what you find to the group?

Reflection

1. When you hear the word "judgment," what is your initial response? How does this response shape your encounter with Revelation? Does the discussion of judgment in this session lead you to think of judgment differently?

2. Focus on Revelation 19:11–16. Consider the many names and other descriptive phrases attributed to the rider of the horse. What features identify this rider as Jesus?

3. Revelation 19:17–21 features the grotesque invitation for the birds to come eat the corpses left over from battle. It also describes the rider of the white horse this way: "From his mouth comes a sharp sword with which to strike down the nations" (19:15). In your opinion, does this image emphasize Jesus's non-violent conquest, or does it attribute violent retribution to him?

4. Can you identify times in your own experience that called for judgment on your part? Do you find yourself resisting the imagery of war and torment featured in Revelation 19:11–20:15? How do you respond to the examples of Martin Luther King, Jr. and Dietrich Bonhoeffer?

5. What do you suppose happens to a person after they die? What have you been told or assumed?

8 | "COMING DOWN OUT OF HEAVEN"

Revelation and the Resolution of All Things

SUMMARY

For many contemporary Christians, Revelation's climax comes as a surprise. No one goes up to heaven; instead, the heavenly city comes down to earth. The New Jerusalem expresses God's intention for humankind and for creation. It also inspires reflection on the nature and value of hope in the midst of hard times.

BASIC BIBLE REFERENCES

Revelation 21–22

WORD LIST

Rapture theology

"COMING DOWN OUT OF HEAVEN"
Revelation and the Resolution of All Things

As we reach Revelation's ending, fearsome judgment turns to glorious hope. The New Jerusalem descends from heaven, as mortals dwell in God's presence. The former things—tears, pain, and death—are no more. "See, I am making all things new" (21:5).

As we study Revelation's concluding vision, we will pay special attention to the book's interaction with Scripture, especially its allusions to Isaiah and Ezekiel.

God's Home Among Mortals

Many readers will find it surprising that Revelation does not end with the saints going up to live in heaven. On the contrary, the New Jerusalem comes down to mortals.

Some of our Christian sisters and brothers treasure an escapist fantasy. According to popular Bible prophecy teachers, Jesus returns to "rapture" true believers, rescue them from suffering, and take them to heaven. Christians escape end-time catastrophes. Revelation knows nothing of this "rapture." In Revelation, believers maintain their faithful witness in the face of intense persecution, risking their lives for the sake of the gospel (12:11).

Revelation fosters no escapism, not even a desire to flee this world. This is God's world. God is committed to it. The first earth does pass

> **No Rapture?**
>
> Many Bible prophecy teachers propound the idea of a rapture. In this scheme, Jesus returns to rescue believers from the devastating judgments of the last days. The Bible prophecy movement has so influenced popular culture that many Christians simply assume rapture theology without examining it.
>
> Simply put, the rapture is not a biblical concept. Bible prophecy teachers take passages like 1 Thessalonians 4:13–17 and Matthew 24:36–42 and force them into Revelation's narrative.
>
> For more on this idea, see Barbara R. Rossing, *The Rapture Exposed* (New York: Basic Books, 2004).

away—and so does the first heaven. A new heaven and a new earth emerge (21:1). God is bringing salvation down to this new earth. "There will be no more night; they need no light of lamp or sun, for the Lord God will be their light, and they will reign forever and ever" (22:5).

A Gated Community?

Many readers complain that Revelation imagines a future in which only a few attain salvation while the masses are cast into the Lake of Fire. Is that how Revelation describes things? The answer lies somewhere between *maybe* and *probably*—and we should add, *it's complicated*.

Three passages in Revelation 21–22 insist that citizenship in the New Jerusalem is exclusive. One passage reminds us that "Those who conquer will inherit these things," but others—ranging from cowards to liars—find themselves in the Fiery Lake (21:7–8). A second passage affirms that "only those who are written in the Lamb's book of life" may enter the city (21:27). A third insists that "outside" dwell the dogs and other sinners (22:15).

On the other hand, Revelation offers some hopeful signs. God makes God's home among mortals in the New Jerusalem, and we learn that they will be God's *peoples*—in the plural (21:3). Until this point, Revelation has referred to the Lamb's followers as a singular people (18:4), reserving the plural for the earth's doomed Inhabitants (10:11; 11:9). Does the plural "peoples" extend hope beyond the Lamb's small band of followers? In describing how God and the Lamb illumine the city, Revelation 21:24 affirms that "The nations will walk by its light, and the kings of the earth will bring their glory into it." The scene echoes the grand vision of Isaiah 60: "Nations shall come to your light, and kings to the brightness of your dawn" (60:3). But wait! Haven't the kings already met their doom (19:18–21)? Moreover, Revelation 22:2 describes the Tree of Life, with leaves that contribute to the healing of the nations.

This language draws upon Isaiah's vision that in the end all the nations will come to Zion and worship Israel's God. As we have seen, Revelation's imagery draws heavily from the Hebrew prophets, with Isaiah prominent among them. The later chapters of Isaiah repeatedly express hope for Israel's relationship to the nations. Consider how the following passages from Isaiah resonate with imagery found in Revelation 21–22.

- Nations shall come to your light, and kings to the brightness of your dawn. (60:3)

- The nations shall see your vindication, and all the kings your glory; and you shall be called by a new name that the mouth of the LORD will give. (62:2)

- For I know their works and their thoughts, and I am coming to gather all nations and tongues; and they shall come and shall see my glory... (66:18)

When we take into consideration Revelation's allusions to Isaiah, we can perceive that John may be extending hope for the nations. Isaiah's vision does not represent a pristine generosity. It also involves "the wealth of the nations" making its way to Jerusalem as kings bring their goods into the Holy City. "You shall enjoy the wealth of the nations, and in their riches you shall glory" (Isaiah 61:6; see 60:5, 11–16; 66:12). Revelation shares in this part of Isaiah's vision as well. "The kings of the earth will bring their glory" into the New Jerusalem (Revelation 21:24).

We cannot ignore the notes of exclusion we encounter in Revelation's closing chapters. But perhaps we can imagine a vision in which grace overcomes even resistance to God and God's purposes, transforming enemies into citizens of the new city.

As for *it's complicated*, readers should keep in mind the social circumstances in which Revelation was written. From John's point of view, society is hostile, dangerous. One believer, Antipas, has already died for his witness (2:13). Others may have lost their lives as well (6:9–11). John himself seems to have suffered (1:9). Moreover, John is not asking the same questions that perplex modern believers. John is not thinking about great representatives of other world religions, like Gandhi, or heroic figures with ambiguous ties to the church, such as Maya Angelou or Abraham Lincoln. John's audience does not enjoy the luxury of abstract speculation concerning such matters. Perhaps that is why the book includes some mixed messages concerning the limits of salvation.

The Resolution of Architecture

Revelation is many things—and one of those things is a story. Revelation sets up a problem: conflict between the Lamb and his followers against the Dragon, the Beast, and their allies. Like most stories, Revelation offers a sense of resolution for this conflict.

For example, Revelation begins with a situation in which all power, all worship, and all wealth apparently belong to the Beast and the Whore. The Beast sits on the Dragon's throne and receives worship (13:3–4). No one can contemplate opposing the Beast (13:4). The Beast controls access to commerce (13:16–17), and it generates so much luxury (18:12–13) that the Whore adorns herself in purple and scarlet, along with "gold and jewels and pearls" (17:4).

On the other hand, throughout Revelation we have heard about God's throne, God's power, and God's abundance. "Worthy is the Lamb that was slaughtered to receive power and wealth and wisdom and might and honor and glory and blessing!" (5:12). But when the New Jerusalem is introduced, the Beast's power and luxury have been destroyed. Instead, the Bride wears fine linen, one of the products in which the Whore had traded (19:8; 18:12). The New City glistens with the radiance of many fine stones (21:11, 19–21). Even its measuring rod is made of gold (21:15). Its walls and streets consist of a peculiar gold that is transparent like glass (21:18, 21). A river runs through the middle of the city, nourishing it and the tree that bears twelve kinds of fruit (22:1–3). The wealth, power, and glory that once accrued to the Beast now reside among the Lamb and his followers.

The point is not (simply) that the New Jerusalem is opulent, that the saints will inherit extravagant wealth. The point is that the unjust conditions that define the lives of the seven churches cannot endure. The sentence, Revelation insists, is just: it amounts to "destroying those who destroy the earth" (11:18).

Revelation also offers resolution in a grander scheme. John did not intend to write the final book of the Christian Bible, but that is how things turned out. Remarkably, Revelation shows more detailed familiarity with the Jewish Scriptures than does any other New Testament book. Revelation avoids quoting Scripture directly, but over and over again it draws words, phrases, and ideas from other biblical books. Revelation is especially fond of the Psalms, Daniel, Isaiah, and Ezekiel. Revelation 21–22 concludes the canon by drawing upon biblical images, particularly Ezekiel's description of a new temple (chapters 40–48). Let's briefly sample just a few of the ways in which Revelation 21–22 draws upon earlier biblical models.

REVELATION	SCRIPTURAL ECHOES
The first heaven and earth pass away (21:1)	"I am about to create new heavens and a new earth" (Isaiah 65:17; see 66:22)
The New Jerusalem "prepared as a bride adorned for her husband" (21:2)	"Put on your beautiful garments, O Jerusalem, the holy city . . ." (Isaiah 52:1) "he has covered me with the robe of righteousness, as a bridegroom decks himself with a garland, and as a bride adorns herself with her jewels" (Isaiah 61:10)
"he will wipe every tear from their eyes. Death will be no more . . ." (21:4)	"he will swallow up death forever. Then the Lord GOD will wipe away the tears from all faces" (Isaiah 25:8)
"I will be their God and they will be my children" (21:7)	"I will be a father to him, and he shall be a son to me." (2 Samuel 7:14)
"It has a great, high wall with twelve gates, and at the gates twelve angels, and on the gates are inscribed the names of the twelve tribes of the Israelites; on the east three gates, on the north three gates, on the south three gates, and on the west three gates." (21:12–13)	Twelve gates for the city, three on each of four sides, all named after one of Israel's twelve tribes (Ezekiel 48:30–34)

Many interpreters have suggested that the New Jerusalem restores the idyllic conditions that were present in the Garden of Eden. One obvious difference between the two is that Eden is represented as a garden while the New Jerusalem is a city. But consider how Revelation draws upon imagery from Eden. Eden includes the Tree of Life, as does the New Jerusalem (Revelation 2:7; 22:2, 14, 19). A river flows from Eden to water the garden just as a river flows through the center of the Holy City (Genesis 2:10; Revelation 22:1–2; see Ezekiel 47:5–12).

The Eden story emphasizes how trees bear fruit, particularly the forbidden fruit of the tree of the knowledge of good and evil; in Revelation the Tree of Life bears a different fruit every month, with its leaves providing healing for the nations (22:2). In the words of Barbara Rossing, "Revelation 22:1–5 recreates the garden of Eden in the center of a thriving urban landscape, drawing on Ezekiel's vision of a wondrous tree-lined river flowing out from the temple" (2013).

John could not have realized while he was writing Revelation that he was also composing the final book of the Christian Bible. John seems to think of books as scrolls. Scrolls were by far the most common form of books in John's day, and Revelation's references to "seals" reflect the conventional method of binding scrolls. John would have encountered Israel's Scriptures in scroll form. The Bible we hold today, however, has a spine and two covers. It begins with Genesis, and it concludes with Revelation. It moves from creation to the new creation, from Eden to the New Jerusalem.

Revelation draws richly upon scriptural antecedents for its imagery. In doing so, Revelation brings resolution not only to the challenges faced by John's seven churches, but also to the entire trajectory of scripture. This pattern testifies that what God has done in and for Israel, God continues to do in Jesus Christ, and God will see to fruition at the end.

Light, Presence, and Hope

In Genesis 1, God's first words are, "Let there be light." John's Gospel calls Jesus the "light of the world" (1:4; 8:12; 9:5). God's light fills the New Jerusalem. The light of God and the Lamb so permeate the new city that it has no need for lamps, no sun—and no night at all (see Isaiah 60:19). Some of us may like the night, but that's beside the point. After John "reveals" the world for its true horror, he describes a world full of divine presence and blessing.

Ecologically sensitive readers have observed the cosmic disorder that haunts much of the book (see Kiel 2017). "Sword, famine, and pestilence" define life under the Beast and under God's judgment (6:8). Earthquakes, polluted waters, and cosmic portents attend the trumpets of judgment (8:7–12). That earth passes away (21:1), leaving us to consider whether Revelation values God's creation or ultimately rejects it. But let us remember that the New Jerusalem is distinctly material. It gleams not only with gold and precious stones, but also with a shining river, "bright as crystal," and with a miraculous tree that bears a new kind of fruit every month of the year (22:2). In the first world, creation has suffered immensely; God's design for the New Jerusalem brings abundance.

Responding to Revelation

Revelation's closing returns to its beginning. John reminds us that he is sharing what he has heard and seen (22:8; 1:1–2). As he does in chapter 1, John falls down in worship, only to be corrected by the angel who attends him (22:8–9; 1:17–18). We learn once again that John's revelation will come to fulfillment "soon" (22:6, 20; 1:1–3, 19). John addresses his audience directly, reminding them (and us) that God's blessing attends those who obey the prophecy (22:14, 18; 1:3), but adding a warning for those who diminish it (22:19). The book ends with longing ("Amen. Come, Lord Jesus!") and with blessing ("The grace of the Lord Jesus be with all the saints. Amen.") The story has come full circle.

Many people search Revelation for ideas. How will history unfold? How does God deal with evil? What lies beyond death?

It's okay to look for information in Revelation, but that wasn't John's primary purpose. Revelation calls for a response. It begins by blessing those who hear and do what is written in the book (1:3), and it concludes by blessing those who do as it teaches and cursing those who do not (22:14–19).

Revelation specifically asked believers in the seven Asian churches to continue following Jesus faithfully and persistently. It required them to abstain from all the trappings of Roman idolatry, to keep their garments clean (3:4), and to "come out" from Babylon (18:4). It invited these believers to testify (12:11) just as John had done (1:9), just as other believers had done (2:13; 6:9–11), and just as Jesus had done (1:5; 3:14; 19:11). It called these believers to risk their lives for the sake of the gospel, and it promised them ultimate blessing if they would endure. After all, Jesus is the *Pantocrator*, the Ruler of All Things (1:8).

Contemporary readers encounter Revelation in a very different context. Few of us face mortal danger for following Jesus. We rarely dispute what we may or may not eat as Christians or what civic organizations we may or may not join. But we do face questions regarding how we follow Christ in the midst of a culture that devalues the gospel while it demeans and exploits people. Daily we must discern how to follow Jesus in a society that asserts other values as more important. Revelation may not speak to our questions directly, and it certainly doesn't answer them all, but it calls for a response from us no less than it did from those vulnerable Jesus followers nearly two thousand years ago.

FOR FURTHER STUDY AND REFLECTION

Meditate

1. Read Revelation 21:1–3 three times, slowly (aloud if you're able). Focus on hearing the words. What images stick in your mind?

Research

1. The concept of the rapture confuses many Christians. If you don't have time to read Barbara R. Rossing's book on the subject, you can watch a video in which she explains how the rapture concept came to be and what is wrong with it. Study groups might want to watch this video together. Search "Rossing rapture" on a website such as YouTube.

2. Revelation 21–22 includes a graphic view of the holy city, one that reminds many readers of Ezekiel 40–48. Other apocalyptic authors provide detailed descriptions of the New Jerusalem or the heavenly realms. After you review Ezekiel 40–48, consider: Why do you think ancient Jews and Christians developed— and treasured—these descriptions?

Reflection

1. Do you ever wonder about the limits of salvation? Do you find Revelation to be consistent or inconsistent on the question of who may enter the New Jerusalem?

2. How important is it to you to have a detailed image of the afterlife? How much are you willing to affirm concerning our eternal hope?

3. Can you describe moments in which you have been especially aware of God's presence? What do they feel like? Do these moments usually happen when you are alone or with others? How long do they last?

4. Revelation ends by blessing its audience—if its audience receives and keeps its contents. Do you find Revelation to be a blessing? Why or why not?

WORKS CITED

Allison, Dale B. 2016. *Night Comes: Death, Imagination, and the Last Things*. Grand Rapids: Eerdmans.

Aune, David E. 1998. *Revelation 17–22*. Word Biblical Commentary 52C. Nashville: Thomas Nelson Publishers.

Bartchy, S. Scott. 2013. "Slaves and Slavery in the Roman World." In *The World of the New Testament: Cultural, Social, and Historical Contexts*, edited by Joel B. Green and Lee Martin McDonald, 169–78. Grand Rapids: Baker Academic.

Boesak, Allan A. 1987. *Comfort and Protest: The Apocalypse from a South African Perspective*. Philadelphia: Westminster Press.

Bonhoeffer, Dietrich. 1971. *Letters & Papers from Prison*. Enlarged edition. Edited by Eberhard Bethge. New York: Macmillan.

Boxall, Ian. 2006. *The Revelation of Saint John*. Black's New Testament Commentaries. Peabody, MA: Hendrickson Publishers.

Carey, Greg. 2022. *Eschatology*. Louisville: Westminster John Knox.

Ehrman, Bart D., ed. and trans. 2003. *The Apostolic Fathers: Volume II*. Loeb Classical Library 25. Cambridge, MA: Harvard University Press.

Evans, Craig A. 2000. "Mark's Incipit and the Priene Calendar Inscription." *Journal of Greco-Roman Christianity and Judaism* no. 1: 67–81.

Fantham, Elaine, Helene Peet Foley, Natalie Boymel Kampen, Sarah B. Pomeroy, and H. Alan Shapiro. 1994. *Women in the Classical World*. New York: Oxford University Press.

Friesen, Steven J. 2001. *Imperial Cults and the Apocalypse of John: Reading Revelation in the Ruins*. New York: Oxford University Press.

Haidt, Jonathan. 2006. *The Happiness Hypothesis: Finding Modern Truth in Ancient Wisdom*. New York: Basic Books.

"Jesus Christ's Return to Earth." 2010. Pew Research Center, July 14, 2010. http://www.pewresearch.org/daily-number/jesus-christs-return-to-earth/.

Jung, C.J. 1954. *Answer to Job.* Translated by R. F. C. Hull. London: Routledge & Keegan Paul.

Kiel, Micah D. 2017. *Apocalyptic Ecology: The Book of Revelation, the Earth, and the Future.* Collegeville, MN: Liturgical.

Lawrence, D.H. 1995. *Apocalypse.* New York: Penguin.

Moss, Candida. 2013. *The Myth of Persecution: How Early Christians Invented a Story of Martyrdom.* New York: HarperOne.

O'Brien, Julia M. 2008. *Challenging Prophetic Metaphor.* Louisville: Westminster John Knox.

O'Leary, Stephen D. 1994. *Arguing the Apocalypse: A Theory of Millennial Rhetoric.* New York: Oxford University Press.

Pippin, Tina. 2012. "Revelation/Apocalypse of John." In *Women's Bible Commentary*, 3rd ed., edited by Carol A. Newsom, Sharon H. Ringe, and Jacqueline E. Lapsley, 627–32. Louisville: Westminster John Knox Press.

Rhoads, David, ed. 2005. *From Every People and Nation: The Book of Revelation in Intercultural Perspective.* Minneapolis: Fortress Press.

Rossing, Barbara R. 2004. *The Rapture Exposed.* New York: Basic Books.

Rossing, Barbara. 2013. "Commentary on Revelation 21:10, 22–22:5." *Working Preacher*, May 5, 2013. http://www.workingpreacher.org/preaching.aspx?commentary_id=1695.

Smith, Preserved. 1914. *The Life and Letters of Martin Luther.* Boston: Houghton Mifflin.

Strawn, Brent D., ed. 2012. *The Bible and the Pursuit of Happiness: What the Old and New Testaments Teach Us about the Good Life.* New York: Oxford University Press.

Wainwright, Arthur. 1993. *Mysterious Apocalypse: Interpreting the Book of Revelation.* Nashville: Abingdon.

Yarbro Collins, Adela. 1980. "Revelation 18: Taunt-Song or Dirge?" In *L'Apocalypse johannique et l'apocalyptique dans le Nouveaux Testament*, edited by Jan Lambrecht, 185–204. Gembloux: J. Ducolot.

Yeatts, John R. 2003. *Revelation.* Believer's Church Bible Commentary. Scottdale, PA: Herald Press.